Frances Bellerby · Selected Poems

Selected Poems

BY

FRANCES BELLERBY

SELECTED AND EDITED BY
ANNE STEVENSON

WITH A BIOGRAPHICAL INTRODUCTION BY
ROBERT GITTINGS

LONDON
THE ENITHARMON PRESS
1986

First published in 1986 by
the Enitharmon Press
22 Huntingdon Road East
Finchley London N2 9DU

Poems © Charles Causley 1986

Introduction © Robert Gittings 1986

ISBN 0 905289 09 9 (hardbound)
ISBN 0 905289 14 5 (wrappers)

BRITISH LIBRARY CATALOGUING
IN PUBLICATION DATA

Bellerby, Frances
Selected poems.
I. Title
821'.914   PR6003.E447
ISBN 0-905289–09–9
ISBN 0–905289–14–5 Pbk

Quotations from the unpublished writings and letters of
Frances Bellerby are made with the permission of Dr.
Charles Causley.

Grateful acknowledgements are due to Marjorie Batt-
cock for permission to quote from Frances Bellerby's
letters to her; and to Mrs Dorothy Shaw for the loan of
photographs.

Printed and made in Great Britain by
The September Press, Wellingborough, Northants

Contents

To the memory of
FRANCES HOROVITZ
who loved these poems

MARY EIRENE FRANCES PARKER was born on 29 August 1899 at St. Aidan's House, Summerhill Road, East Bristol. Her father was the Reverend F. Talbot Parker, who came from a large, provincial doctor's family in Weymouth. He had met his wife, Marion Eirene Thomas, daughter of a Bristol solicitor, at a seaside parish outing during his first curacy, which was at Clifton in Bristol. Like him, she was exceptionally handsome; tall and dark, her colouring, looks and temperament were inherited by her blue-eyed daughter. Mr Parker was an ardent and 'Socialist' Anglo-Catholic, with a mission to the poor, 'possessed', as his daughter wrote,[1] 'by powerful desire to take under the authority of the Church the gospel to the poor and by it to comfort the sick and dying. He had no wish whatsoever to bother about the rich.' His wife, who, after being educated at Clifton High School, trained as a nurse at the London Chest Hospital, Victoria Park, shared his faith, and threw herself into his parish activities. He soon moved to the missionary 'Tin Church' of St Aidan's in the poor, working class area of East Bristol, a parish in the coal belt of collieries, worked-out quarries, streets of terraced cottages running down to crowded slums. His ideals of service coloured all his daughter's early years. They had no carpets or curtains in their own house, and only the most rudimentary furniture.[2]

The Parker family – a son, Jack, had been born in 1896 – were exceptionally tight-knit and isolated socially, the sole island of middle-class, among the 'poor, poorer and poorest'. Though rich sympathizers from other parts of Bristol provided for a proper church, which the children saw built, 'Few children live as isolated a life as we did in our nursery

[1] MS Autobiography.   [2] *ibid.*

9

years.' In such an existence, with hardly any toys except two discarded surplices, everything was loved with a kind of sacramental ardour especially when connected with her mother. 'I was born a sacramentalist'. Every evening her mother read to her.[1]

> My mother would be ready for me in the little square room at the top of the stairs . . . . I am in the dark little passage with the front door behind me. The light which I see above me streams through the fanlight above the front door and through the windows of upstairs rooms . . . . I reached the top step, breathless and eager, and found my mother ready seated by the table in that square glory of light.

In her old age, Frances commemorated such moments in a poem, 'The Room'.

> 'Child! Child! Come along in!
> Old Sun's at downfall,
> time you were in bed,
> or you'll miss the light on the wall
> that you so love.'
>
> 'I came in long ago.
> I never miss the light on the wall
> that I so love.
> I never shall.'

While everything about her mother, even a certain yellow vase Frances gave her, acquired the nature of a sacrament, Frances felt her brother Jack as a hero-figure. Also tall and handsome, as spectacularly blond as she was dark, he treated her as the brother he had wanted, teaching her to box as his sparring partner, and actually to be his second in fights.[2] Until her early twenties Frances looked like a boy. The children walked with their governess, a curious glimpse of middle-class distinction in such an area; their favourite

---

[1] MS Autobiography.   [2] Frances Bellerby to Marjorie Battcock, n.d.

play-place was in a field just at the end of the tramway, where open country began, with a big pink chestnut,[1] again recollected by Frances in a poem of her old age, 'Brother and Sister'.

> Would you say that field is the one?
> Look, my dear, there's the great
> pink chestnut, and the straight path
> from iron gate to iron gate –
> the old sort, that you wind yourself through.
> Yes, that field is the one.
>
> Then the tree's shadow must still make a tent.
> What are we so troubled about, the two of us?
> There's shelter, freedom and the whole of time
> whilst the slow sun follows its long course,
> and in and out of the shadow-tent play,
> those deathless children, to our hearts' content.

To emulate and be like this brother was another total passion. 'I did not want to be pretty. Prettiness was for girls!'[2]

The atmosphere of intense idealism and self-sacrifice at home, combined with social isolation, set her life in a pattern of intensity, which was not lessened until she was well past school age; 'at 22', she later wrote, 'I hadn't begun to get used to the normal.'[3] Up to the age of nine, she was taught by her mother: she wrote poems for her from the age of three or four. At nine, after knocking down a local boy in a fight in the churchyard, she went to Mortimer House School, Clifton, an Anglo-Catholic private school where her fees were remitted by the influence of an Anglo-Catholic vicar. Home-taught, she found herself more advanced than girls three years older there. Her brother was already at Clifton College, paid for by a rich godmother. The well-to-do district of Clifton was the other end of Bristol from her father's parish, so she lodged till the age of 13 in a 'happy term-time home' of friends, who

---

[1] MS Autobiography.   [2] FB to MB, n.d.   [3] MS Autobiography.

appear in detail in her only novel. At first treated, perhaps understandably, as 'an oddity', she grew to adore school, where she remained till she was nearly 19; but the extra-ordinary obsessive unity of the family was maintained. 'We *were* as four; to me as-it-was-in-the-beginning-is-now-and-ever-shall-be.'[1]

Yet the vigorous 'Public School lines' on which the school was run found her an over-zealous disciple too.[2]

> . . . there was perhaps rather over-encouragement of the Spartan attitude. This perfectly appealed to me . . . I did deliberately overdo the Spartan, went for a training run every spare half-hour, got up at 5 to swim, then (breakfastless) worked in a squad mowing, rolling, marking the beautiful Games field, played cricket all the evening, got home at 8 often worked till twelve.

Contrary to most girls, she was heart-broken when, on leaving, she could no longer wear the school hat. One could get a wrong impression from this kind of enthusiasm – 'Games were a part of religion' – and the fact that in late life she would use disconcertingly hearty schoolgirl expressions, 'jape' and 'kybosh', She was vulnerable, sensitive, and had a tremulous inner life. Her feeling for animals was a passion of pure instinct towards the snails, tortoises and other unlikely companions of her room. When she saw an old man strike a donkey with a spade, she wanted to kill him.[3] Then from the age of seven till her death there was the Flying Dream, which combined ecstasy and energy, an easy sensation of floating along above ground level, or sometimes varied to form the dream of flying and diving, where she plunged safely down from cliff-tops to harebell-coloured sea.[4] Above all, 'my awareness of the tremendous, dwarfing-all-else, value of poetry was part of my childhood.'[5] Among the main peaks of family unity were the summer holidays all four took

[1] MS Autobiography.
[2] FB to MB, 11 September 1968.
[3] MS Autobiography.
[4] *ibid.*
[5] FB to MB, n.d.

together. 'Something lives, while I live, of every summer holiday in my life.'[1] Many of these were in Cornwall, at least before the First World War, and took place in seaside houses lent by richer friends or relatives.

In 1913, they were too busy for a holiday. Her father, for long 'perpetual curate' of St. Aidan's, with no hope of preferment, had just been inducted Vicar of Holy Nativity, Knowle, another district of south-east Bristol. This move, in spite of his larger stipend and enjoyment at the time, became a symbol of disaster for Frances. Knowle was 'where our lives broke'. This was not owing to the place, but to the associations it acquired in their family life. The next year, the War broke out. Her brother Jack, who had left school early to enter an uncle's bank in London, was eighteen. He at once volunteered, giving his age as 22, and, too impatient to wait for a commission, enlisted as a private in the Cold-stream Guards. On embarkation leave in 1915, he calmly told his father he knew he would be killed, and that this would be better than returning maimed. On Sunday 8 August 1915, a brilliant summer day, he was blown to pieces in France.[2] Frances always regarded this death 'which I saw through tears, as absolute perfection' in the light of a triumphant fulfilment of his own wish; but, though they heard the news on their first family holiday without him, in Devon, the shock was associated with Knowle. Secondly, at the end of the war, her mother, affected by the menopause, began to collapse under the accumulated strain of parish work. Frances blamed her father for lack of understanding, and was at loggerheads with him herself. 'There are many older people who automatically are antagonistic to those twenty years younger. (My father was one of these).'[3] This too she associated with Knowle.

Knowledge of this failure of relationship between her mother and father shattered, as she afterwards wrote, her

[1] MS Autobiography.   [3] FB to MB, 11 February 1967.
[2] Typescript Autobiography.

13

whole world in her early twenties. There were difficulties too about religion. Like everything else a passionate affair with her, in her childhood she '*could not bear* what they had done to Jesus', and late in life still could say 'What a relief that Holy Week is over'.[1] In her late teens, however, she embraced pantheism, and in her twenties, though still a communicant, she was repelled by some Anglo-Catholics and their ritualism, seeking herself 'the simplest and least ornate' form of worship.[2]

Yet though in retrospect the decade of her twenties seemed horribly darkened by her mother's spiritual and mental ill-health, 'which *only I knew*', Frances nearly always regarded it as a time of happy experience. A close friend wrote, 'This period was about the calmest and most pleasant in Frances' life'. On leaving school in 1918, she trained for a year at an animal kennels, going daily from her home at Knowle. The lady owner must have been an exceptional teacher. All Frances's observations on animals are notably lucid, scientific and accurate. From 1919 she herself taught English, Latin and games for a year or so at Luckley near Wokingham in Berkshire, the 'daughter' of her own school, started by her former housemistress. She enjoyed this experience immensely. She spent her holidays at home, and there, in Bristol, two events gave her the greatest pleasure. The local paper, *The Bristol Times and Mirror,* which had a high standard, accepted her articles, which the editor began to use regularly. Secondly, a branch of the great local family of Fry, the Cecil Frys, gave her the living-in job as home-tutor to their three children and the children of some of their friends. Here again, she was supremely happy, as she also seemed to have been on her out-of-term holidays. She spent a memorable one in summer 1925 at Lulworth Cove, with a former pupil from Luckley. In the fine weather, she indulged her passion for swimming – she also saved her friend from drowning – and wrote poetry. About this time, she was

[1] FB to MB, 10 April 1971.   [2] *ibid*, 25 November 1970.

engaged briefly to a family friend, connected with her brother. Since just after the War, he had annually written her a letter to arrive on 8 August, the day of her brother's death. Though their engagement did not last, these letters continued for 50 years till her own death.

1927 saw a revolution in her life. Impressed by her work, the editor of *The Bristol Times and Mirror* offered her a staff job in the paper's London office, in Hen and Chicken Court, off Fleet Street. She was their dramatic critic, doing four or five plays a week, of her own choice. London was a wonder to her. In old age, pain, and unhappiness, she could still write of this time, 'I *loved* London. Heavens, how I loved it!' She walked all over Town at night, often all the way from her office to the unfurnished flat she shared with a friend from Luckley at 7a Courtfield Gardens, near Gloucester Road tube, 'climbing 81 stairs to the tree-top flat'. Her friend, slightly better-off provided the furniture, 'the happy hunting-ground for both mice and clothes-moths'.

There were also the literary delights of living in London. The P.E.N. Club had been founded in 1921. In 1928, the Young P.E.N. was founded for young writers, 'who had not, perhaps, had any of their work published, but who, nevertheless, are sincerely writers.' It was inaugurated on 4 October, at a meeting where Galsworthy took the chair, and E. M. Forster spoke. Frances attended, was introduced to Galsworthy, and wrote ecstatically to her mother, 'My right hand is not the same as it was. I've shaken hands with Galsworthy.'[1] In her limited spare time she did voluntary work as 'Book Young Lady' at the poor law hospital, St. Peter's Whitechapel: 'I begged, borrowed, stole, bought if necessary and went to every bed.'[2] In the course of these years, she met again a remarkable man she had first encountered in 1925 during her memorable summer at Lulworth Cove, where he too had been a visitor.

[1] FB to MB, 14 August 1974.   [2] FB to MB n.d.

John Rotherford Bellerby[1] was the son of a Yorkshire businessman. The same age as her brother, he had like him joined up in the First World War while still very young, serving with distinction, gaining the Military Cross, and suffering the loss of an arm. He returned to take a brilliant First at Leeds University, and to an appointment in the International Labour Organisation at Geneva, where a series of studies on banking and unemployment established his reputation as an economist. In 1927 he became a Fellow of Caius College, Cambridge, and Frances visited him there in the summer of 1929.[2] She discussed with him an organisation he planned to found, called The Neighbours, and the problems of modern society. They spent days out of doors, walking, swimming at Byron's Pool, lying at the edge of cornfields, accompanied always by her beloved wire-haired terrier Sheila. On 9 December 1929, they married at Kensington Registry Office. The two had a 'wedding breakfast' in a Whitechapel eating house near Toynbee Hall, where her husband lodged. It consisted of sausage and mash: Frances, being a vegetarian, ate most of the potato, and gave her husband the sausages.[3] The marriage was, he later said, 'for maximum contribution' to their work,[4] but it became clear she was very much in love with him ; she later wrote of 'its passionate joy and misery.'[5]

Meanwhile, she must further the scheme they had in common. The Neighbours, which she herself described in a brief pamphlet in 1931, was a small, voluntary spare-time organisation for general social welfare. Both in her husband's work, and in the mind of the nation, the misery of unemployment was the chief factor at the beginning of the 1930s. The Neighbours was one of the many idealistic, though highly theoretical attempts at that time by middle-class intellectuals to awake a social conscience at the plight

[1] *Times*, Obituary 5 April 1977.
[2] MS Autobiography 2.
[3] FB to MB, n.d.
[4] Note Book No. 0.
[5] Note Book No. 4.

of the poor. As an economist, Bellerby tried to give his scheme a logical and practical financial slogan. 'Every penny saved is a penny more to give.' Members were to live on the national economic 'average wage', £3 when single, £4 for a married couple. The surplus saved from their normal earnings was put into a trust for education, in particular for an educational press. It would be hard on members, especially married women. Bellerby himself confessed in print[1] 'for my wife it was virtually ostracism'. Looking back, Frances Bellerby thought it 'in some way *inspired*'. Yet, as she also explained[2]

> If one received a present, its value had to be calculated as taken from what one permitted oneself to live on. Likewise if one had a meal at anyone else's expense, etc. etc. It made a very strange and rather niggling affair of daily life from any social point of view. In the case of illness, it could and sometimes did make harmful hardship.

She had only been married six months when cruel disaster overtook her: as she believed 'the accident that has ruined my adult life'. It was a spinal injury, culminating, after much agonising vicissitude, in a condition known as ankylosing spondylitis, with complete fusion and stiffening of the whole back. In her case, this deformity was eventually accompanied by almost continuous pain and difficulty in moving. Yet it arose from an apparently absurd and casual incident, 'a moment's damn-fool idiocy.'[3]

In June 1930, she and her husband spent a camping holiday on the Dorset cliffs at Lulworth, accompanied by another couple. Always exhilarated by the sea and swimming, she was running at full speed on the cliffs when her husband tried to catch her. Handicapped by his missing arm he failed to do so, and she fell heavily on some rocks. She felt at once that she was badly hurt, though she pretended not to

---

[1] J.R. Bellerby, *The Conflict of Values* (1933).
[2] FB to MB, n.d.   [3] Note Book, No. 3.

be. 'I saw . . tall golden letters: THIS IS FOR EVER' Thinking she was all right, her husband went down to the shore with the man-friend, while she, unable now to control her tears, dragged herself along the ground to their woman-friend, who 'told me of someone who had suffered terribly from a fall like that, *20 years after* I knew I should too.'

The real pain started a month later. Her account of treatment for it is confused, largely because she snipped out of her note-book a passage which obviously deals with deficiencies of the doctors and the medical profession in general. She also seems to be hinting that there were gynaecological complications. At all events, she was now crippled, in one way or another, for the remaining 45 years of her life.

Unfortunately the 1930s were not a good time for the treatment of spinal injury. Frances Bellerby afterwards regretted she had not 'gone to a doctor, a good doctor . . . after the accident' in 1930. In some ways it may have been lucky she did not. When in 1936 she at last allowed 'an elephantine doctor' to manipulate her spine, he only succeeded in adding to the lumbar or lower-spine injury some complications in the upper part of her spine.[1] Manipulation at that time was often of the crudest 'Swedish drill' kind; it was even sometimes applied on the principle that if exercises caused pain, it was a proof they were effective. Frances Bellerby, on the contrary, noted of an enforced laying-up in 1932, due to another illness, 'Perhaps the rest was good for my injury?'[2] At any rate, it seems to have given her a year's respite from pain. It seems possible that simple rest would have eased the early part of her 45 years' intermittent agony of body. She herself found a sensible relief by taking gentle exercise with the lower part of her spine supported. She went swimming, using her arms only, continuing this till 1940. She seems also at times to have worn a spinal jacket, though these too were often very crudely made of steel and leather.

[1] Note Book, No. 4.   [2] *ibid.*

The 45 years' agony of her mind was difficult to deal with. One of the most distressing features of spinal trouble is the acute depression that accompanies it. This is all the deeper when the sufferer had formerly been athletic, and takes a joy in physical skill. Nearing the end of her life, Frances Bellerby pathetically recalled her school-day triumphs; 'Captain of Cricket, Captain of Hockey, Swimming and Diving Colours, a cross-country runner.' Her images are often taken from athletics, with an exactitude of description in both verse and prose.[1]

> The leaders in the vast formation of starlings hurling across the sheepdog sky, seem to reach an appointed place – a post in the air – touch it and turn back all in one movement (like a perfected turn in a Swimming Bath) . .

Self-confessed, she had no patience, could not suffer fools gladly. Illness made her temperament worse.[2] Frances Bellerby could not bear being clumsy. It infuriated her when she had to be helped physically. She burst out[3] in 1951

> I HATE my spine. I am going to write this here because I want it out of me. I HATE my spine . . . I am NEVER used to it. I NEVER shall be . . . I NEVER shall be reconciled to *this*.

She saw 'my body as a millstone round the neck of my spirit',[4] though it was not until 1956 that she began to see herself in dreams as disabled. Until then, she had always dreamt of her former athletic self.

Meanwhile, in 1930, this untoward injury was not allowed to interfere with her social work. Whatever talents she had shown in journalism were to be harnessed to The Neighbours. 'Look here,' said her husband, 'You write a book about the kind of school we really want, where people grow up wanting to blow the East End sky-high, and build

---

[1] Note Book, No. 5.
[2] FB to MB, 27 January 1968.
[3] Note Book, No. 2
[4] Note Book, No. 4.

something beautiful in its place, and don't mind *how* much they spend themselves in the attempt. Write it as a novel.' 'All right,' she said, 'I'll try.'[1]

So to order, but with obvious love and enthusiasm, she wrote *Shadowy Bricks*. It is hardly a novel, but a 'Progessive' 20th century version of the Victorian Sunday School tract, its title taken from Humbert Wolfe's poem *The Teacher* – 'shadowy bricks of innocence'. It describes a progressive school for children of 5 to 11, in the Dorset countryside. The young teacher represents Frances Bellerby's adult self: athletic, romantic, a child-lover, grieving over her inseparable dog's death, searching for an undoctrinaire religion, feeling compassion for the poor and sick. 'Stella saw God shining in everyone she met.' One child seems to be the author in childhood, 'most intelligent, sensitive, imaginative, agonizingly shy.' The book appeared late in 1932, and received an enthusiastic review in the *Times Literary Supplement*.

Just before the book appeared, her life had received another shattering blow. Her father had retired from his parish in 1927. Her mother's health had finally broken down some years before. Their lives were not happy, and they could not decide whether to live on in Bristol, or move to Winchester, where Mrs Parker was always more relaxed, as Frances noted, living near her married sister there. Frances visited her from time to time, and received her mother's confidences about her father's lack of understanding. In 1930, when at Winchester, Mrs Parker was severely ill, and had two internal operations. She emerged in an acute state of depression, which persisted. Back at Winchester in 1932, in the same house where they had stayed before, her husband left her one afternoon. He returned to find the bedroom door blocked with furniture and the room full of gas. She had committed suicide.[2]

Frances Bellerby later wrote 'her suffering could only be

---

[1] *Shadowy Bricks*, jacket blurb, 1932.   [2] *Hampshire Chronicle*, 9 July 1932.

ended by my forcing my way into it with her, at whatever cost'. She added 'I suffered and broke and died with her.' Certainly her own life was approaching a crisis, which may account for a later comment on her parents' lives – 'Their tragedy has been my tragedy.'[1] In autumn 1930, Frances Bellerby's husband had been appointed Brunner Professor of Economic Science in the University of Liverpool, where they went to live. Her educational tract, *Shadowy Bricks* (1932), was published with a foreword by the Bishop of Liverpool. She had not been long in Liverpool before she experienced what she always described as 'my long illness.'[2] The illness, which was for some time suspected to be tuberculosis, caused the enforced rest which gave her some relief from her spinal pain; this had returned almost directly they went to Liverpool. It is also clear that the strain of living up to her husband's organisation, The Neighbours, was telling on her. It was probably with her in mind that he himself wrote of

> the psychic strain in living always differently from their immediate friends . . . during illness the trouble is worst.

He added, percipiently, and perhaps with some self-reproach,

> It is often to the highly-strung sensitive type, least capable of withstanding strain, that a regime of self-exaction makes most appeal. A heavy responsibility rests on any member of the group if he allows or persuades another to join who is of this character.[3]

Frances Bellerby was all-too-clearly of this type. The strain on her was increased by a change of direction in their lives. Deciding that the real social danger was not unemployment but the threat of war, Bellerby, for reasons never fully explained, threw up his professorship in September 1932, and retired to a cottage at Bourn, a small village with a

[1] MS Autobiography, No. 1.
[2] Note Book, No. 3.
[3] J.R. Bellerby, *The Conflict of Values*.

famous windmill a few miles north of Cambridge. He joined the Oxford Group (ancestor of Moral Rearmament) and was adopted as a pacifist Labour candidate for Cambridgeshire.[1] Though he later abandoned pacifism for rearmament against Hitler, he stood as Labour candidate in the 1935 General Election, polling as many votes as the previous Labour man, but failing to unseat the Conservative member.[2] She shared his pacifism, and in 1934 became a Quaker, because of 'the Church's failure in principle, practice, or speech where war is concerned.'[3] In a condition of great stress after her mother's death and her own illness, on 29 February 1934, and feeling, as she afterwards confessed, 'temporarily insane', she told Bellerby they ought to part. To her dismay, he took to this all too readily,[4] and they had a short unhappy interlude when she lived alone in south-west Cornwall. This arrangement did not last; but, looking back, she was convinced they should have separated permanently then. She had not written any poems since their marriage in 1929, and came to believe that, had they parted in 1934, poetry would at once have returned. As it was, they continued to live largely together for eight more years, and no poetry came. Shortly after her husband's unsuccessful candidature, they lived for two or three years in a caravan in a friend's field at Eastbury on the Berkshire Downs, together with her pets, 'a monkey and 2 cavies' (South American rodents). Later they put up a wooden cottage, thatched, and she ran a small animal clinic in the caravan.[5] There were a few brief holidays in Cornwall, mostly in the coast between Fowey and Falmouth: and suddenly, in 1941, alone in a Cornish cottage, poetry returned, unpremeditated, after a total of '12 lost years.'[6] She put it down to an unaccountable feeling that her 'inner self' had become *free of him*', though even then they did not formally part for another seven years.

[1] *Times*, obituary.
[2] Whitaker's Almanac.
[3] FB to MB, 19 February 1962.
[4] Note Book, No. 0.
[5] FB to MB, 28 November 1969.
[6] Note Book; No. 3.

Bellerby returned to academic life in 1942 as Lecturer in Economics at Glasgow, going on to a distinguished career on the research staff of the Institute of Agricultural Economics Research at Oxford, where he became a University Demonstrator. He continued to be in touch with her, and sent her copies of his books as they came out.

The return of poetry came in some sort of physical emanation, as she recalled in old age. 'I remember very clearly the Presence in the lamp-lit room, the tremendous, deep, still excitement, the immediate writing down of the dictated words.'[1] Since summer 1940, she had been living at Plash Mill, Upton Cross, near Callington, a thatched, white-washed building by a stream overlooked by Bodmin Moor. One of its attractions was that it was near places where she had spent many childhood holidays with her family before the War. Looe, where they had been for successive summers from 1908 to 1912, was barely a dozen miles away. She still felt estranged from her father, confirmed in this by the malign influence, so she thought, of a mutual friend in 1938,[2] and the other two were dead. Yet now she began to relive their former happy life. The 'lost years' had at any rate been productive of prose. Her notebooks are full of anecdotes, conversations, information, designed to help her write 'the perfect short story'.[3] She had published a volume of stories, *Come To An End* in 1939; they are uneven, the best being those which are most autobiographical. Now she sent her poetry to her agent, and, to her surprise, he placed this too in various magazines, especially *The Listener*, where the poems attracted very favourable attention. It was a time of great production for her. She took up a half-finished novel, *Hath the Rain a Father?*, completed and published it. She never considered herself a novelist, and did not rate it highly, though it sold well; but its publication in 1946 gave her the idea of collecting her poems too. They

[1] FB to MB, 5 August 1970.   [3] MS notes on writing poetry.
[2] Note Book, No. 5.

Plash Mill, March 1943

came out next year. Entitled *Plash Mill*, the book was well
reviewed.

The place itself was a seed-ground for writing – another
book of stories, *The Acorn and the Cup*, also largely autobio-
graphical, appeared in 1948. In her notebooks, the theme is
the great natural beauty of the place, observed with minute
intensity. The birds rattling and creaking in the thatch, the
honeycomb pattern of the low sun on her bedroom wall, the
'stutter' of the water in the stream, the white owls at dusk
filled her life. She was alone but did not feel lonely. Her
companions were the small farm children, who used to come
and talk to her, and into whose lives she entered. All 'that life
behind the appearances of life, which, I think, was once in
some way known to me' returned to render her a fresh calm.
She seemed '*to know things out of time.*'[1]

---

[1] Note Book, No. 2.

This knowledge is reflected in the prose of her notebook entries, especially those in the year 1950, when she had been at Plash Mill for nearly ten years. In March she wrote

The colour of the steeply rising ploughed field seems to reflect in the whole day. A delicate shining, March day, of a peculiar *fawn* colour, almost a *sand* colour. There is pink in it. I have seen that field under snow, and under grass, year in year out, and under the heavy, violet, wet winter earth. I have seen the great carthorses flourish and play there, shining, grey and bay. And the red heifers, brilliant in the evening, their shadows long before them. And the jackdaws ink on gold, and the shadows of birds running up the tall dividing hedge.

Next month, April, there is an entry.

In the night, which was still not very dark, a small bird sang, suddenly, a bar or two, then no more. It was 3.30 a.m. S.T. This is the third time in my life that I have heard such a thing. The second time was only a few weeks ago. I think that one wants to live under old and broken thatch. This third time I seemed to be aroused from a very shallow sleep by the sound, so close was it. It might have been a chaffinch – I found it strangely unidentifiable, alone, and with almost, I thought, that curious other-worldly quality that a sleeping voice has.

Next month, there is the single entry, 'The bird again'.[1] In August is the entry which gave the title to the book of poems she published this same year, *The Brightening Cloud*.

The colourless pale sky, the dramatic darkened iron-coloured east; over the cottage roof, as though leaning from the high moor's edge, the huge magnificent flame-coloured cloud. And as I stare up, it grows & grows & spreads like a fire across the overhead sky.

It is the last entry before a dramatic and terrifying change in her life. All through the year, 1950, she had been suffering from pain across her breasts. This was diagnosed as possibly

[1] Note Book, No. 2

25

a twisted muscle, caused by her spinal condition. Suddenly there was acute pain, and on 27 September she was rushed into Lamellion Hospital, Liskeard, for operation on what was thought to be a large cyst in one of her breasts. 'The shock was still to come – five days later – the diagnosis.'[1] There was cancer of both breasts. It was decided to give her a course of deep X-ray therapy, postponing the decision about further operation. Three times each week in the winter of 1950-1951, the hospital car fetched her from Plash Mill to the radio-therapy unit for Out-Patients at the Plymouth Greenbank Hospital. Winter weather is severe in East Cornwall. Sometimes she was driven back by the direct road through Callington, sometimes along the coastal road to Liskeard, then north up the valley to Upton Cross. The exhaustion from the therapy resulted in terrible alternations of mood between blackness and light. 'Is there a Tormentor?' she wrote on 9 January 1951, yet comforted herself somehow by quoting Christopher Smart's words on his cat Jeffry

> For when he takes his prey he plays with it to give it a chance
> For one mouse in seven escapes by his dallying

Not so much her own suffering, but the tortured appearance of other out-patients, '*burnt away* by cancer' affected her. After one session she broke down in front of the doctor, an incident of which she was bitterly ashamed, though re-assured by kindness at her next session.[2] The evening drives back to Plash Mill, whether by Callington or Liskeard, provided visions of skyscape and seascape, which, in her weakened state, were like revelation; but now Plash Mill, in its lonely hollow of shadow, reached after a long, exhausting day, seemed tomb-like. 'Plash Mill has not lately seemed to me "a good place to come back to"'; though beautiful, it seemed 'too still'.[3] Only her farmer's children, who cared for

[1] FB to MB, 19 August 1972.   [2] Note Book, No. 2.   [3] *ibid.*

the cottage and her pets in her absence, reconciled her to it.[1]

The condition showed no improvement under treatment. 'An internal growth was found, diagnosed as inoperable cancer and I was . . . given perhaps a year perhaps about five months'.[2] She was moved into the chronic ward in Lamellion Hospital, but while there, a new surgeon, who examined her, gave her new hope. After a further small operation, 'he asked if I would let him do a big exploratory operation, as he was doubtful of the former diagnosis'. For the first time for months, she had a glimmer of hope, even in those surroundings.

> There is *no hope* in this ward. I am the person with hope of ever getting out, and I myself am often frantic with the feeling of being trapped.

All her notes on other patients and the nurses are full of sympathy: for the old, mad Russian woman, or the patient with claustrophobia, who tries to escape, carrying her handbag. The operation took place at St. Barnabas Hospital, Saltash, in the first week in June. 'The cancer *was* operable'. On 15 June, the surgeon told her there was a chance it had been successful – 'an extraordinary kind of exhilaration possesses me', though she remembered his warnings against over-optimism. She was moved, later that summer, to two nursing homes for recuperation. 'And now I am living. I am not at present, dying.'[3]

In her own mind, Frances Bellerby felt that she had 'died' during the operation in June 1951. 'I died then', she afterwards wrote.[4] She regarded herself as a Lazarus, who had experienced real death and return to life, and who now lived in that knowledge of death. She wondered if 'I' were dead, and life now 'my dream, or perhaps someone else's dream.'[5] Very slowly indeed; this entered her poetry, and became an essential part of it in the two-dozen more years

[1] FB to MB, August 1967.
[2] FB to MB, 19 August 1972.
[3] Note Book, No. 2.
[4] Note Book, No. 3.
[5] FB to MB n.d.

she was destined to live. Its most complete expression is in this poem, written between 1970 and 1973, twenty years after her operation.

Lazarus dare not raise his eyes
above the hooded valley.
Dare not level his weak sight
with that flooded glory.
Death-black on crystal clarity
a coast line there
edges a wide estuary
of primrose water fair
and smiling as though nothing had to die.
Time displaying eternity –

This peace and loveliness
Lazarus cannot share,
nor that most gentle shadowless
further honey-gold shore
detailed there in light:
rock-bound pools, sand,
shallow coves beneath kind
woods which lie deliberate
as gentle beasts at rest,
sun-yellow in that shadowless
light unseen by Lazarus,
death's brief departed guest.

So there'll be no recall
of this first evening of his resurrection
except by touch of grass
cool to the feet – and quickly then
blackbird's loud rattling call.
It will be this and this
that store for Lazarus all
his dazed and trembling bliss,
his charmed and freshened life
brilliant with death, the ratified
lord of his heart still safe,
still uncrucified.

The images used in this poem are almost inexplicable, until one looks at Frances Bellerby's hospital journals.[1] Here is one of her entries after being driven back, from her therapy treatment, from Plymouth one evening on the Torpoint-Liskeard road on 23 February 1951.

> Have I ever seen anything more wonderful than the sky this evening . . . ? it was unbearable to me.

Like Lazarus, she cannot bear the vision, which she nevertheless records.

> Low in the west the sky was an amazing yellow, the sun above it being quite hidden in a blue-black cloud . . . Later in Liskeard, the vivid almost *lemon*-yellow light . . . the flat jig-saw puzzle bits of grassland on the estuary's mud-flats are the colour of a camel.

When Lazarus does return to life, after having been unable to take in the 'flooded glory' of this vision, of the estuary shore, the colour of a camel, which has suggested her 'gentle beasts at rest', Frances Bellerby recalls him to life in terms of her own experience, noted while recovering from the operation at the second of the two convalescent nursing homes.[2]

> And then, on the morning of August 6th, to walk on grass again, to brush my hand through wet grass. Now this was a thing I had thought never to do again. I had thought, in hospital, and in the Home, with intolerable anguish of longing, of wayside grass . . .

There was only one drawback to this sense of resurrection in 1951. Plash Mill had become for her associated with the tomb, from which, like Lazarus, she had been saved. Her returns from therapy to its quiet and shadowed dark had oppressed her. 'The silent, dark & tomb-like hollow of my home' she had written more than once. It was the 'hooded valley' with 'light unseen' of her later poem. It may also have seemed too physically isolated and mentally lonely. On an

---

[1] Note Book, No. 2.   [2] *ibid.*

impulse, when she was still in the Nursing Home, elated at being alive, in July 1951, she answered an advertisement for a cottage to let at Clearbrook, Devon,[1] on the south edge of Dartmoor, a move she almost at once bitterly regretted when she went there later in the same year. She felt herself totally unable to write there, though she also attributed this temporary state to the shock of change wrought in her by the operation. 'The pen is mightier than the sword, yes, but not than the surgeon's knife'. As for Plash Mill, she was poignantly reminded by a visit from the children from the farm there, now growing up, who paid her a visit. 'Plash Mill was truly their second home; & I was *never* lonely because they were always coming . . . I almost laughed again today.'[2]

In actual fact, life was not so unlaughing or sterile as her self-tormenting notebooks make out. All through the 1950s, her poems were broadcast frequently by the BBC West Region radio, introduced by Charles Causley whom she had met in 1950 after poems by both of them had been included in a programme produced and compiled by J.C. Trewin. In 1953, John Lehmann broadcast a poem on the Third Programme, which he later included in *The Chatto Book of Modern Poetry*. Poetry had not, as she feared, been stopped by the surgeon's knife. Not only was her output of new poems steady, but these nearly all dealt with the events just before, during and just after her operation. She wrote poems based on her journeys in the hospital car, to and from Plymouth for radiation treatment: in the chronic ward in Lamellion Hospital, where she had been before the major operation itself: on the 'liquid fire' of pain during convalescence, when she was denied morphia: on the relief of finding herself still alive. Most of the poems use actual phrases, written at the time of these events, in her notebooks, even quoting stray lines that she had jotted down.[3] Many are built around her resurrection as Lazarus from the grave in June 1951. One short poem is significantly entitled *Dying in June*. The

---

[1] Note Book, No. 3.   [2] Note Book, No. 2.   [3] *ibid.*

collection of these poems, printed by a Plymouth bookseller-publisher, emerged in January 1958[1] and was dedicated to Charles Causley. In 1952, her last collection of short stories, *A Breathless Child* had also appeared, and had been reviewed by Causley on BBC West Region. It is an astonishing set of a dozen stories, once more carrying with them, as he noted, a strong stream of autobiography, some from her recent experiences, most from deep back in her life. The reviewer found them almost unbearably poignant.

The poems too are more concentrated, firmer, and stronger than much that she had previously written. *The Stone Angel and the Stone Man*, in spite of an unfavourable review in the *Times Literary Supplement*, is the collection in which she began to find her true voice; much of the diffuseness and over-writing which weakened her previous work has begun to drop away. There is even a wry sense of humour, which appears in the ironic-titled *Your Guess is as Good as Mine*, with its adroit rhythms and half-rhymes.

It occurs to me that in darkness Soul goes well,
Leaping like a firefish,
Diving like a star, crammed full
   Of godly artifice.

But that Body stumbles whenever left without light,
Mind stammers,
Until each, becoming aware of the other's plight
And heeding rumours

Of devilry, crumbles with fear, and betrays
His onetime friend
In a crazy cracking hope to save
The beginning from the end.

Whilst all the time Soul speeds on through the darkness,
Firefish, star.
To forget those inadequate companions? I'd guess
Just gently to remember.

---

[1] Frances Bellerby, *The Stone Angel and the Stone Man*, Ted Williams, Plymouth.

If the mid-1950s were a time of poetry, they also signalled two great changes in her life. Early in December 1954, her father died in Bristol. She visited St. Aidan's for his Requiem Mass and funeral service. Waking early on the day of his burial, she had a vision of the perfect early-morning sky, which seemed to make it 'all, all, not only bearable but right, perfect'.[1] Less bearable was the arrival, next month, at her home in Devon of all the relics of her mother, which her father had kept for over twenty years since her suicide. They even included the wooden name-board from her mother's coffin. These relics, going back to her mother's nineteenth year, were so unbearable to her that she burned most of them, 'the scores of marked & written-in books, the poetry, the prayers, the devotions.' She felt shattered by the experience, hardly able to remain sane.[2]

On the other hand some relief was afforded by moving house again. She had never felt happy during the three and a half years at Clearbrook. Her father's death now left her just enough money to buy a house for herself and not rely on rented property. In 1955 she bought a semi-detached cottage called Upsteps at Goveton, a small village near the town of Kingsbridge, Devon, where she lived for the remaining twenty years of her life. Though she never ceased to regret having left Plash Mill after her operation, this at first seemed a fresh start. As she walked, in spite of her disability, through the midsummer hedges of the winding lane to Kingsbridge, 'I saw and felt, as my old self did, my real self that accompanied me all my life, unchanged, unchangeable.' The birds flew in to be fed at her ever-open kitchen window. One sign of a temporary return to peace of mind and well-being was her passionate interest in her pet animals, visiting them 'in my little bit of garden here, stepping over the threshold of my always-open back door with a timeless feeling of freedom.' She described in minute detail one of the females of her five tortoises laying eggs, and it took her back to the days of Plash

[1] Note Book, No. 3.   [2] ibid.

32

At Plash Mill, about 1950

Mill, where she had first bought the tortoises. The Raeburn stove was always kept in, to make it warm enough for them to breed, and 'we know one another by heart'.[1] The lizards made a home in her wastepaper basket, watched by an attentive whiskered circle of kittens. She realised that if she had been a vet, as she had wished to be when 14, she would not have written poetry because 'they use the *same* juice. They are, and have been since infancy, *the absorbtion* of my entire being'.[2] On the other hand, her successful breeding of tawny Oak Eggar moths provided an image which recurs throughout her later poems.

This respite of comparative happiness did not last. Ever since the beginning of this year 1955, when her mother's relics arrived after her father's death, she had been haunted by their family past. This was joined to the conviction that

[1] Note Book, No. 3 and FB to MB, 11 September 1968.
[2] Note Book, No. 3.

she herself, at the time of her operation, had really 'died', like Lazarus. Now that she was the only living member of her family, she saw all the others as real, including her own young self of 11 or 12 years old. It was her present fifty-five-year-old self who was really a ghost, and who could not get in touch with the rest.[1]

> The happy talks the laughter will go on,
> the river runs smooth as a blindworm
> under the bank, it is all *perfect and forever*.
> But *I* am outside. I have no part of it.
>   They are all dead. I live. It is I
> Who am the ghost.
>   Is there anguish greater than this?

She had an urgent need to 'get back' somehow to the three members of her family, who were dead yet living, and to her 'dead' but living self in childhood. She determined to attempt an autobiography, which would recapture that early life. It would recreate her brother, father, and mother and continue for just over thirty years until the time of her mother's suicide in 1932. It was to be a reassurance to herself, *A Pebble in the Pocket*, as she intended to call the whole book, after an earlier title was abandoned, 'a pebble in the pocket on which the hand automatically closes in moments of stress or in abeyance'. Partly it was to help, in some way, her mother: to alleviate the tragedy of her mother's life. Even more broadly, 'my hope is that the writing of this book, if I am able to write it, may pacify my entire living memory.[2]

At first she wrote with enthusiasm. She began sketching the book on 22 September 1957. After many revisions, she typed two introductory chapters, a very long one on her parents, a short one on her brother, totalling nearly 20,000 words, and sent them to Charles Causley in 1959. He greeted them with appreciation, only suggesting some shortening, to bring the projected book into proportion.[3] Yet from then

[1] Note Book, No. 3.   [2] Typescript autobiography.
[3] Charles Causley to Frances Bellerby, 11 January 1959.

onward the book became a struggle. After five more years, in 1964, she was still 'writing my autobiographical book (which endangers my mind & body).' In that year she confessed that the book was still all rough draft so far, except the introductory chapter', and added ominously, 'It's rather *dangerous* work.'[1] In 1965, she wrote of the pain it would cause to revise certain episodes. 'It draws blood at every touch. Can I live through it?'[2] The preliminary chapters were constantly revised. She added long speculations on the nature of memory. There were passages to be interpolated, and she did not seem to know where they should go. The first 'introductory chapter' runs to 55 typed pages. The 'rough drafts' of the main book in all these years, hardly get beyond the immensely-detailed recollections of the first nine years of her own life. Outside that, there are only some stray passages about later life, consisting of a few pages about her mother, and a few about her own husband: but these, as soon as they tend toward painful episodes, abruptly break off. Her brother's death in 1915 is introduced, but very little that occurs after it. The year, 1966, when she had been at work, on and off, for no less than eight years, is the last time she mentions writing the book, which 'continues to bring on violent attacks of illness.'[3] In 1968, she wrote to a friend about giving up the arduous attempt.

I am not really considering working again at my autobiography . . . I have some fear of insanity . . . I meant in this book to go down into hell with one whom I loved.

This was, of course, her mother, for it was partly to enter into her mother's tragedy that she had begun the autobiography. Now she felt that, even to 'help' her mother, long-dead, she dared not go on with the book.[4]

There were additional handicaps. In summer 1957, just before starting the book, a new kind of physical pain assailed

[1] FB to MB, 11 February 1964.
[2] Note Book, No. 4.
[3] FB to MB, 11 September 1966.
[4] FB to MB 27 January 1968.

her. Years before, when a kindly doctor had asked, 'Does your back hurt?', she had answered automatically, 'My back hurts, and my hip hurts and my neck hurts, most things hurt.'[1] Now she had an alarming form of attack, which persisted for the rest of her life. It was a circulatory trouble, intermittent claudication, causing intense cramp-like pains in arms and legs, and leaving all her limbs weak. She became even less mobile, could hardly walk out of doors except with two sticks, and eventually found she could not type. She experienced alarming spasms.

> The blood stops flowing in various parts of me; the pain following is out of the region of the bearable. Also, one's heart keeps threatening to stop, then at what feels like the last moment the blood comes with a violent rush . . .

In one attack 'an egg-shaped wheel whizzed behind my eyes, the world began to go dark.'[2]

There is no wonder that during the 1960s, her poetry fell off both in amount and quality. The strain of the autobiography, and the alarming stress of the new disease, both worked against it. There are desperate entries in her notebooks. 'Desolate. Desolate. Desolate. Frightened, broken, alone' – and again, 'I do not know where I am.'[3] Terrifying dreams ravaged her nights. She later wrote, about poetry, 'for me, my whole lifetime it has come from stress, from what would be unbearable without poetry to "make sense" of it all'. Yet in the same breath, she draws a distinction between this 'stress' and what she calls 'chaos'.[4] Her 1960s were a time of annihilating chaos. She thought the new disease was playing cat-and-mouse with her, and reverted to the fears of her operation days, that there was 'a Tormentor'. She felt 'the Holy Ghost' had deserted her. She prayed, often without

[1] Note Book, No. 2.
[2] FB to MB, n.d. and 12 September 1965.
[3] Note Book, No. 4.
[4] Frances Bellerby to Alan Clodd, 6 August 1971.

success, to be 'sent an angel' to succour her.[1] Deeply religious, she prayed too each night for 'all prisoners and captives; all sick persons and young children; animals . . . '[2]

She made a will of pathetically small individual bequests to friends, the important provision of all her books, MS., typescripts and notebooks to Charles Causley, and 'all my tortoises and their various houses to Paignton Zoo.'[3]

In some sense, the 'angel' which saved her was her continuing effort to write poetry. She became more self-critical of past work. For instance, in August 1968, she took up a poem printed in the 1958 collection, and completely rewrote it. Originally called *August Night*, it had been about the death of her brother on 8 August 1915. Every year, at this date, she said, that 'experience *goes on happening*', not as a mere memory.[4] This August, she revised the previous poem, which was muddled and inconclusive, with echoes of G.M. Hopkins, and refashioned it into a new poem, first called *Anniversary*, then simply *1915*. It opened with a line borrowed from the original version

Never mourn the deathless dead.

'The deathless dead' were now to be her theme. Having failed, in the autobiography, to face entering into the lives of her dead, she now wrote poems demonstrating the timeless nature of those lives. At this point, Charles Causley sent a copy of *The Stone Angel and the Stone Man* to Alan Clodd, of the Enitharmon Press, and suggested a selection from her previous books, which he would edit. In 1970 appeared her *Selected Poems*. It was dedicated 'To the brief and everlasting life of my brother'. Henceforward, the timelessness of all experience was to be her dominant note, and a supreme comfort to her.

---

[1] Note Book, No. 4.
[2] FB to MB, n.d.
[3] Frances Bellerby, will drawn 14 August 1963, Somerset House.
[4] FB to MB, 14 August 1973.

Though sales were small the reception of the book, by Kathleen Raine and others, inspired and reassured her. In the next few years, 1970 to 1973, she wrote a considerable cluster of fresh poems, all of a new vital quality. In these late years, she had jotted down some brief notes, intended perhaps to be printed as an article, on her own poetry. Her aims, with age, had become clarified throughout. 'I now want my poems to be good secretaryship. I want to write down what I hear & see & no more & no less.'[1] Yet this did not limit these later poems, but simply confirmed how immeasurably she had improved with the years. Her earlier poems had sometimes been criticized for being too diffuse, too rhetorical. Her late poems are pared down to a point of tremendous force in very little space. Even the occasional long poem is intensely concentrated, in expression and feeling.

Her poems at last seemed to succeed in sharing the life of those dear to her, and now dead. The ten-year struggle to do this through her autobiography had been abandoned because it 'endangered' her peace of mind and even her reason. Somehow, her poems could establish contact more peacefully, and could fulfil her 'when I cry out to God, or not to God. . "Oh I want to go *back* to them. ."'. One of her deepest needs was to feel reconciled with her father, to be forgiven by him for her part in their estrangement: for him to know 'that I now *understand, and that the bad years don't count.*'[2] This reconciliation emerged as a short poem.

> When the sun goes into the wood
> we shall end our day.
> Will the whole journey be understood,
> step by step of the way
>
> Re-travelled, as your hand and mine
> part, for the last time
> forgiven and forgiving? . . . O then shine,
> unrivalled, light from home!

[1] Loose MS. notes, untitled.   [2] Note Book, No. 5.

In old age at Goveton, early 1970's

Outside the timeless life of poetry, her days and nights are still full of terrifying visions and dreams. Her health was further deteriorating, and it seemed in 1972, as she sometimes feared, that the twenty-year remission from cancer might be ceasing.[1] This proved to be so, and, in fact, she eventually died from a return of breast cancer. Meanwhile, there were many difficulties and domestic worries. Charles Causley and others suggested she should apply to the Royal Literary Fund. This she did not do, partly because she feared tax complications – she was already receiving alimony from her ex-husband.[2] In 1973, however, kind influences procured her a small pension from the Civil List, for services to literature.

By 1974, she had collected enough for another book, which Alan Clodd was to publish under the title, *The*

[1] FB to MB, 19 August 1972.   [2] FB to MB, various dates.

First-Known and Other Poems.[1] She wrote 'this certainly gives me a strong wish to live through the winter' and 'how extraordinarily good to me he is.' The title-poem shows a calm acceptance, very different from the agony of life she poured into her note-books.

> I am free to come and go –
> That is the bargain I have made.
> The door stands wide. Is never closed.
> The threshold's worn by me and the dead.
>
> When the wind rages, and the rain,
> hurled half-across the impassive room,
> streams down my lifted face like tears,
> I hear the calling of my name
>
> Tossed in the tempest, here and there,
> by that immortal first-known voice
> – my friend, my lover, my unseen
> gaoler in this hidden place.
>
> One day, one night, one dawn, one dusk,
> I will call back, not hesitate,
> nor search my memory, heart and mind,
> for that dear Name. But still not yet.
>
> Freedom's my chain. Take that and give
> truth. Uncloud my hindered eyes,
> unstop my ears, that once for all
> I see, and hear, and recognize.

On 28 July 1975 a copy of the newly-printed book was put into her hands. She had dedicated it to her mother,

> Because of the beginning
> and because of
> an end
> which was not after all
> the end.

Two days later, Frances Bellerby herself died.

[1] FB to MB, n.d. and 21 May 1972.

Her final poems had done what she attempted but failed to achieve in her autobiography, in which she had written[1]

My desire is to state explicitly the terms of the complete transformation which has come about for me in the essential significance of the past. It is as though, having gone a long distance out of sight of the vision of my childhood, having witnessed the desecration of all that I had believed to be viable, and having watched everything on which my eyes had dwelt with love tortured, twisted, made hideous and unrecognisable with agony – I had at last lost consciousness. Regaining it after a long and most strange interval, to find myself destitute of all – except the vision with which I began.

[1] Typescript Autobiography.

Checklist of the published writings of

Perhaps? (essays) London : Fowler Wright, 1927. Under the name of Frances Parker.

The Unspoiled (long short story) London : Fowler Wright, 1928. Under the name of Frances Parker.

Shadowy Bricks (novel) London : Education Services, 1932. A note by the author in her copy states that the book owes its conception to J.R. Bellerby and that several passages, including almost the whole of Chapter X, are his work.

The Neighbours London : Richard Clay, 1931. A pamphlet in the Education Services series.

Come To An End and Other Stories London : Methuen, 1939.

Plash Mill (poems) London : Peter Davies, 1946.

Hath the Rain a Father? (novel) London : Peter Davies, 1946.

The Acorn and The Cup with Other Stories London : Peter Davies, 1948.

The Brightening Cloud and Other Poems London : Peter Davies, 1949.

A Breathless Child and Other Stories London : Collins, 1952.

The Stone Angel and The Stone Man (poems) Plymouth : Ted Williams, 1958.

The Stuttering Water and Other Poems Gillingham : Arc, 1970. Wrappers. Limited to 200 copies including 25 numbered and signed by the author.

Selected Poems Chosen and introduced by Charles Causley. London : Enitharmon Press, 1970. Limited to 300 numbered copies including 45 specially bound and signed by the author and Charles Causley.

The First-Known and Other Poems London : Enitharmon Press, 1975. Issued hardbound and in wrappers; specially bound limited issue of 45 copies.

Selected Poems Selected and edited by Anne Stevenson with a biographical introduction by Robert Gittings. London : Enitharmon Press, 1986. Issued hardbound and in wrappers.

Selected Short Stories Selected and with an introduction by Jeremy Hooker. London : Enitharmon Press, 1986. Issued hardbound and in wrappers.

Ephemera

Son of the House n.d. (?1960). Issued by the author as a greetings card and reprinting a poem from Neville Braybrooke's anthology *A Partridge in a Pear Tree* (1960).

Contemporary. Issued by the author in December 1970 as a Christmas greetings card. Reprinted from *Selected Poems* (1970).

A Possible Prayer on New Year's Day. Issued as a greeting card for New Year 1972 by the Enitharmon Press.

In Memory of Frances Bellerby n.d. (1975). Issued by the Enitharmon Press in September 1975. Prints two poems *The Silver Sea* and *Light.*

NOTE

In so far as is practicable, the poems are printed chrono-
logically in the order in which the individual collections
appeared. In one or two cases I have changed the order in
accordance with my own feeling about their place in the
present context. The poems from *The Stone Angel and the
Stone Man* were originally arranged in reverse order of
writing i.e. those written first appear towards the end. The
title poem itself was written in 1956, two years before
publication.

ANNE STEVENSON

FROM
Plash Mill
(1946)

Voices

I heard those voices today again:
Voices of women and children, down in that hollow
Of blazing light into which swoops the tree-darkened lane
Before it mounts up into the shadow again.

I turned the bend – just as always before
There was no one at all down there in the sunlit hollow;
Only ferns in the wall, foxgloves by the hanging door
Of that blind old desolate cottage. And just as before

I noticed the leaping glitter of light
Where the stream runs under the lane; in that mine-dark
    archway
– Water and stones unseen as though in the gloom of night –
Like glittering fish slithers and leaps the light.

I waited long at the bend of the lane,
But heard only the murmuring water under the archway.
Yet I tell you, I've been to that place again and again,
And always, in summer weather, those voices are plain,
Down near that broken house, just where the tree-darkened
    lane
Swoops into the hollow of light before mounting to shadow
    again . . .

Invalided Home

He is coming back.
The child would retreat only under protest,
But the man will come without protesting.

Will he come to stay?
Here, deeply at-home, he could perhaps rest,
At last content with resting.

Here he could lie,
Listen to the stream, and easily forget
The discipline of forgetting.

Not a single voice
Of the water would be new. He would hear
Conversation he was used to hearing

As a child in bed;
Would understand, mind luminous with dream,
As the child, half-dreaming,

Understood the whole thing.
And would soon, like the drowsy child, accept
All that needs accepting.

*   *   *

But do you think he will stay
Even as long as the daffodils out there
Under the apple tree –
Brushed tenderly
On the frost-grey grass and the translucent air
This opening day?

February Again

Gnat-like dances the small rain . . . .
Green chalice of the lupin-leaf cups crystal drop again;
There, a naked sycamore branch gleams like a snake;
Silver as Christmas the spangled grass-blades shake;
While gnat-like jigs and dances the sweet small rain.

In the unlustred air,
Neighbouring that sunshine flare
Of gorse whose golden triumph no tempest can deny
Though every April flower unborn should die,
The timeless bracken's sodden flame burns deep,
Memory of autumn sleep,
In the unlustred, gentle, silver-spattered air;

While gnat-like jigs and dances the sweet, small, silver
    rain. . . .

Summer

In spite of all this undeniable evidence
It may be wise not to forget
That the dazzling glory of summer can scarcely influence
The inquisitors of the spirit.
Sentence may come with any breath
To living death.

A tree is nothing but a tree to the living dead,
And light's silver dance
High overhead
Merits no wonder, and no second glance.

A stream is flowing water to the living dead.
No need to listen;
To be overheard
No intimate loveliness of conversation.

And if the wind comes from the sea to the living dead
By some million-flowered way,
No eyes are blinded
With tears – there is here no cause for ecstasy.

Safest perhaps to ignore the profligate exuberance
By concentrating with care
On some minute detail of summer perfection. For instance
One might study to share
The godhead of this lemon spider on buttercup petal,
His frail felicity
Enfolded by insect's and flower's mutual
Profound simplicity.

The Intruders

Oh, look at that little house! There must be ancient secrets
Kept by so still a tongue. Deep down, deep in the hollow
    evening,
Deep in the waveless grass under those heavy trees;
Pale, in the silent cavern
Of water-green light
Crouched.

Shall we go down? ... No one here. . Black beams, broken
    stone floor.
Strange, the vibrating air in such old empty houses
Suddenly entered! What could have been going on?
In this fuscous, stone-smelling room
What did we
Interrupt?

Why tremble? Why need to pretend there's some reason
For glancing around, alert for the sad green window,
Brightly alert for anything save the silence,
Anything? ... Yet there is only
The false silence
To be heard.

Are you *crying?* But though men are strangers here now
Life flows on. Look, the grasses lean through the broken
    pane,
And dandelion seeds from their little full moon by the door
Float along these passive walls
Where spiders live
And die.

But oh, because of your tears we will go away from here
And never come back. Because of your cold hand
    comfortless
In mine. Perhaps you are right, and we are not wanted
    here,
And the silence waits for us
As we came
To depart.

Departure Postponed

1

Here once more is the brilliant confusion of summer!
I had not thought to behold again
The buttercups, and the tall red luminous sorrel,
The wiry-stalked grasses shaking the light in their flowers,
And the kingly host of foxgloves in purple splendour
Down the quarry slope
At the wood's edge.

Here once more is the wind-flung motley of fragrance!
I had not thought to smell again
These thousand flowers – hawthorn – mountain-ash;
Sun-battered water and stone and timber and earth;
Green-ness; and faint over meadow and woodland and
        moor,
Tangy, elusive,
The summer sea.

Here once more is the exquisite disorder of birdsong!
I had not thought to hear again
The countless cuckoo-game of cup-and-ball
At the first glint of dawn; and then the spreading
Out, like a fan, of the vast orchestra:
Anarchist singers
In heedless accord.

2

Now butterflies dance; and dances the light
Like a tree-netted shoal of fish
High over the cottage roof
In the tossing foliage.

Now flutter, unsettled, the wings of light,
Hesitant, wavering, delicate,
Over the deep orchard grass
And the moss-yellowed bark of the trees.

Now from the chestnut horse glows burning light,
The fly on the leaf is a jewel,
The thistledown hair of the child
A pale torch at the cottage door.

3

Oh, here once more is the tearing anguish of sorrow,
The bitterness!
I had not thought to prepare again for departure,
Cry another Hail and Farewell; for all was accomplished;
The agony past, away had I turned, quiet-footed,
And should before now
Have gone very far.

The Summer Dove

There was dazzling sunlight on the day of my friend's
    funeral,
And the parson's surplice bellied like a sail in the summer
    wind.
I remember thinking: What a heavenly day for a burial –
As I heard about beauty like a moth-fretted garment,
About grass, and flowers, and fleeing shadows,
The glory of the sun, and immortality.
Beautiful words I caught at the funeral service of my friend,
Fragment of a sentence here, and there another fragment,
In the summer wind tossed so lightly
And sent far adrift like thistledown over the shining
    meadows.

But I wanted to laugh with my friend at the absurdity
Of all that dire solemnity
Where all the black-rook mourners and the magpie parson
    gathered near the hole in the ground!
Whilst a lizard panted on the wall near-by,
And I caught an interested robin's bold appraising eye.
Then I grew drowsy with a dove's perpetual, soothing,
    cool and leafy sound.

Walking home by the field-path after my friend's funeral,
Aware of the indefinable singing of the summer day,
I thought: Well, everything goes on as usual,
After all the dead can never be so important
As the living; it is Life that is warm and urgent,
And Death certainly can claim no victory
For where's victory when whatever you touch simply
    crumbles away?
And for crumbling, what so appropriate as a hole in the
    ground? . . .
Then I grew drowsy with a dove's perpetual, soothing,
    cool and leafy sound.

Since that was how things happened yesterday
It seems strange that today
Hearing the cool-voiced dove I am suddenly blind in my
      pain,
Blind and wrung with the piercing of my sorrow . . .
And I must hear, oh I must hear the summer dove again
Tomorrow, and tomorrow . . .

Night and Morning

The coldness is not forgotten, the loneliness,
Nor the long, detailed anguish of the hollow night,
Nor that lunatic zig-zag of laughter in the darkness –
Mind mocking heart; – and then the creeping light
Without colour, without lustre, without gleam,
Grey and still as a dream.

The flowering grass is not forgotten – the tawny steam
Shimmering above the wall in the first sunshine;
Nor the air, like thin gauze hanging, beyond the stream
In the cavern of trees; nor the single crystalline
Larch-feather curving clear; nor the gate's vast shadow
Lightly drawn on the meadow.

Strange

'Look, oh, look!' . . . 'Where?' . . .
'There, down there,
Quickly!' . . .

'I see
A million leaves, yellow, yellow as new pennies –
Like some fantastic snowstorm they stream slanting
Down as the wind goes suddenly prancing
Along the valley. . . . Now I see whirling flurries –
And a score of leaves dance mad as cats on the road
      there! . . .
It's the sudden wind makes them do that, I swear –
That's all it is, you know . . .'

'Up here where we stand
Is not a breath of wind;
Glass laid on the lips of the day
Cloudless would stay.
Quick, oh quick, let us go! . . .'

Plash Mill, Under the Moor

The wind leapt, mad-wolf, over the rim of the moor
At a single bound, and with furious uproar
Fell on the tree-ringed house by the deep-cut stream –
Quiet little house standing alone,
Blind, old, pale as the moon,
And sunk in some ancient grassy dream.

Through all the roaring maniac din
Outside, the shadowless stillness there within
Held. No face, all the frantic day,
Pressed the glass, watching the green apple hailstorm,
No child's heart gladdened at thought of where acorns lay,
And beechnuts, treasure for harvesting safe from harm.

Now, firewood in the ragged grass will waste, sodden
Under the winter trees; and the darkening apples lie hidden;
And the driven leaves at the door stay huddled in vain,
Or, death-brittle, float on the floor under the broken pane.
But when, next March perhaps, sunlight the colour of frost
Wavers through branches to honeycomb some flaking wall
Changeless since autumn, that will be the utmost
Hope realised: light's delicate miracle
Of grace
Still wrought on the forsaken place.

What Then?

Men never come this way. In winter
The steep lane is a stone-jagged stream.
Leaves lie in deep drifts
Tawny-orange, fulgent;
Flattened leaves, brilliant, cling to the water-barrel,
One or two still slashed with sharpest green.
The lichen-furred branches of the apple-trees
Without movement criss-cross the sad white sky
Whilst in those clear frail heights of the seven beeches
Ink-shapes of rooks sway gently, far-away
As childhood.
          The single flower of red campion
Under the sky-broken hedge careless lives on.

Men do not come this way. The fact is common knowledge.
Two rattle-voiced magpies see-saw and jerk on a branch;
Tinkling, the tits fly in and out of a window;
Robin bounces, looking in sideways through a pane;
Mild weather stirs Hedgehog from the shed's dark corner –
He pats out of his leaves and rags to snuffle and rootle
Round the grassed edges of the silent house;
Sometimes, in snow-magic days, featherfoot Fox
Appears in the orchard, and thinking himself unwatched
Suddenly flings up his heels, leaps and bounds,
Laughing and wild and dark on the tell-tale snow;
Always the lissom mice are busy at home
In the house; Rat, living under the water-barrel,
Often shoots up, and, forepaws on the rim of his hole,
Waves his head this way and that, delicately vibrating,
Looking like a parson in a pulpit, about to preach. . . .

Men do not come this way. The leaf-patterned grass
Seems likely to have its will for ever now,
And the broken gate swing on in the yellow wind,
And bright holly berries make annual festival
For mice and birds, but never mysterious gleam
In dark-and-silver rooms.

        The fox-red bracken on the wall,
Flogged low by ancient angry weather, will burn
Unquenchable, unchanged through many seasons,
Timeless, forgotten. . . .

        This whole place has been
Forgotten, I think; – is a part of someone's past,
Part of some childhood now obscured
By the strange thick dream that life becomes
As we live on. Surely there's someone groping,
Struggling with muffling veils, baffled by half-glimpses
Caught from sight, scent or sound. And at last, in the
      moment of dying
Perhaps, the struggler will break through,
      return. . . . Then what of me
The homeless one in this place, shy guest of a night
      unended,
Traveller exhausted by the deadweight of hope, who took
      shelter
Here; and, accepted, stayed on, stayed on,
Never discovering, never,
Any way out? . . . Oh, what then of me
When the native returns to his home?

Prayer for a Dying Brother

Lord, may his eyes remember
The vagaries of light
At play with wind and water
All day! and the jewel-glitter
Of leaves and grasses! The bright
Beetle's rust-red shimmer!
And let his ears remember
A thousand harmonies
From the song of our endless summer! . .

Though even this rain's broad ivy-clatter
And the creaking groan of the black stark trees
Might be comfort, Lord, for him to hear.

Night

Behind the silence is sound,
Rhythmic orchestral background:
Chuckle rattle thud of winter water
Swirling hurling, froth-sudded brim-levelled, after
Dark-faced weeks of rain.
Now sharp-blade yelps the owl close by;
Again; and, further off, again
Although without softest whisper of flight –
And at once the moonlight-frozen night
Hollows undinted round the sword-slash lightning-flash cry.

Am I the dreamer or the dream? . . .
There's something now half-heard
Under the winter symphony of the stream,
And close behind that shock of flashing cry –
And now in the hiss of rain's quick violence.
Not a sound in silence leaves the heart undisturbed.
But *what* do I half-sense?
Someone commenting? Calling?
Who? Is it I?
Or am I myself called, from far, always too far, away,
The voice lost swiftly as a wild star seen falling, falling,
Like the bright brief ghost of a shot bird? . . .

Drive Home from Hospital

There rests the dusk-brown country
Grave and still.
What should disturb the sleeping heart
If that were all?

But trees stark-delicate as bone
And black as jet
In absolute precision stand revealed
On flaming light.

And the smooth rampart of hills
Dark in the west
Cannot hold back the radiant clouds –
Soaring, vast,

Like giant shapes of amber smoke
They billow across the sky. . . .
Now the road is bordered with liquid light
Though it twists away

North. . . . Now another turn
Heads for the hill
Looming near and black against glass-green light,
The clearest light of all,

Making it seem that a hollow green world of light
Just over the rim of the hill
Must be the goal of the heart's cruel journey home,
And the end of all.

Whose Hand?

When the lamp burns dim
And the fire is sunken,
And in my midnight house
The long quiet day has shrunken
To the last sliding grains of sand –
Then, for an instant touching mine, whose hand?. . . .

Cool as daffodil, as moth-wing light,
How can so frail a touch be strong to blind the sight,
Strangle the throat, defend the pounding ears,
Pierce the astonished heart to pour its tears?
Never in my life has any touch so done –
And whose hand can reach me, where I am – alone?

When I move to take the candle, by the sinking firelight
I see another finger crooked, and in faint lucent line
Another hand, and all at once the crocus flame stands bright
Although no light has yet been made by these two hands of
    mine. . . .
Who kindles light for me? Not in my life has this been done –
And whose hand can be here, where I am – alone?

Who Could it Be?

Just now, those strangers walked past my gate –
Not for the first time, nor the second –
On the rough Old Road, seldom used except by me.
And again I saw them hesitate,
Start, glance this way as if I had called or beckoned
Urgently.

I held my breath until a torrent of light
Came pouring out of the west behind me
Making them flinch, turn dazzled; half-afraid,
Half-sure that their first idea was after all right,
And the desolate place as silent as it should be,
And as dead.

Now they have gone. But again they'll come strolling past
I think, and again start and turn, fancying a cry
As if there were someone imprisoned here, held fast,
Who must, at the strange rare sight of a passer-by,
Shout for help, wave from the window, desperate
To be heard, to be seen – oh, tomorrow may be too late! . . .

But who could it be?
For there is no one here with me.

Lovers are Separate

'Do you hear the bells?'

'What bells?'

'The swinging bells the singing bells
Downed bells drowned bells
Hear the flying sound the dying sound
Tossed sound lost sound
Of the old bells sea-cold bells
Under the sea.'

'Bells? I hear nothing
But the even breath of the sea.
And look, oh come closer and look with me –
From this rock we stare down into depths so clear
We should see any bells that might be there.
No, there is nothing.
Only the chrysoprase water, deep,
Making a large, bare, twilit room
Such as I've wandered through in sleep,
A dream home . . .'

'Yes; but I tell you I hear the bells ringing!
Almost, I see the wild swinging
And then the swung sound the up-flung sound
Balanced high aloft – high aloft – listen now, right overhead!
Hear it top-
            -pling stumbling sliding and tumbling
All down the silver air into the green sea
To be lost.
Again lost
As the dead
In that hollow sea.

'And still you heard nothing?'

'Alas, we could not have drawn closer and yet I
        heard nothing
But the even breath of the sea.'

Aged Thirteen

Pierced by bright Pain, last night I died.
Then mourners stood at my bedside –
I watched the piteous sight
By yellow candlelight.
And whom there did I see?
Not Father nor Mother,
Not Sister nor Brother,
But Strangers three!

Loudly I called asking them who they were –
But my young Angel hurled the window wide
And caught me to his side –
Across the violet sky streamed his fierce golden hair
Whilst upward, on, we swept through all the blazing night,
Sinking at last to emerald meadows of delight. .

But who *were* those strange three
Weeping last night for me?
What did I hear them say
Ere my strong Angel swept us on our way?
One swayed with long young hands over her eyes;
And one, a child, clung to this weeper's sleeve;
The third, with little mumbling broken cries
How she did grieve,
Her wrinkled apple face fallen loose with sorrow!
Ah, did I hear them cry
As my fierce Angel leapt into the sky,
'Oh bright, oh bitter Pain!
    We too, we too, are slain,
        For we were this dead child's most sweet tomorrow'?

FROM

The Brightening Cloud and Other Poems

(1949)

The Old Ones

In the May evening
Flowing with golden light,
Out went the old woman
To meditate;

Pottered through the orchard,
Her cat at her side –
So old the two of them,
Time they died.

But when they sat them down on the bench
Under an apple tree,
'Here we are', said the old woman,
'Where we belong to be'.

Blossom floated from the branches,
Light as snowflakes touched those two friends,
Coarsened fur and faded hair
And bent transparent hands.

So they sat, the two of them,
In some content . . . .
The violent bats swerved to and fro,
The brightness went,

Leaving the sky as any shell
Delicate and pure;
Soundless flitted past the moths
Through the dim blossomy air.

Yet still, still, those old ones –
As if the sun still shone –
Sat there, never noticing
Another day had gone.

'Here we are', said the old woman,
'Under the apple tree
'On this sweet May evening,
'Where we belong to be.'

Plash Mill

No stillness in the burning
Sun and moon,
Nor in the travelling
Starshine,

Nor where the fierce root writhes,
Nor where change storms in the seed –
Transmutes the sapless leaf –
Breathes through the dead;

Neither is stillness in water;
Nor in stone.
Where, then, save
In the unfleshed bone?

Not even there; for it seems, to a quiet hand
On this wall's breathing stone
May flow the greeting of another hand,
Three centuries unfleshed bone.

Night that the Dead have Loved

Night that the dead have loved, in whose
Silent, dim-silvered space there flows
Calm life of stone, water and wood –
What of the starless throbbing solitude
Prisoning madman, criminal?
What of the lover's terrible
Reluctant dying? And oh, that utmost fear
Of those wild trapped for whom sunrise despair
Must be sole anodyne? . . .
There's night enough for all.
But this calm flawless life in water, wood and stone,
This deathless way of Life, this gentle miracle? . . .

Very Early in the Morning

Shall the chained heart despair?
The dead rot in the grave?
Again the hour of dawn comes near,
The kingdom of the Sun's love.

Oh, the lissom waters are wine, of that bright kingdom,
Its shining stones are bread;
There, there, the prisoner, finding some childish freedom,
Laughs, and is enchanted
By what was once thrown away;
And there, at the dawn of every day
All grave-clothes, done with, lie neatly folded.

No one appears more important there
Then any other:
Every shimmering beetle inhabitant there
Shows God and His little brother
Clothed and imbued with the same fanciful light,
Taut with the same purpose, aristocrat,
Poet, workman, and lover.

Shall the chained heart despair?
The dead rot in the grave?
Now is the hour of the dawn, and here
The kingdom of the Sun's love.

Death in the Snow

Then, our dear Lord the Sun having died,
I begged the Fox: 'Have you a hole?'
But Fox stared far with snow-mad eyes –
Each of us alone, alone.

So I knelt in the snow by a death-dwindling Bird.
'Let me be your nest, small Son of Life'.
And I gathered that brittleness close, lest there lurk
In its hollows faint dust of Light.

Oh, futile claws to savage the air,
Piteous wings beating my breast!
But deep in the eyes what fierce lamps flared
To blind the eyes of Death!

Ah, vain: with one loud cry, sweet Bird,
Disowned, lay dumb, lay still. . . .
How gently then, between sky and earth
Slid apricot light, wafer-thin

And smooth! And forgotten shadows of trees
Stroked the kind velvet snow!
Lifeless, deathless, I could but kneel
Watching this light that flowed

Out from no visible worldly Sun,
No vehement glittering Lord;
Whilst all the time the snow-clouds hung
Waiting in the north,

And Fox, in the spell of that dreadful cry,
Over the velvet snow
Stared back, the flame from his death-mad eyes
Scorching the eyes of my soul.

The Ultimate Reality

A stranger came to my door,
Said: 'Here am I'.
But over his shoulder I watched ten buzzards
Swing circling in the opal sky;

Swing, crying, near and nearer
Until they traced, right overhead,
Curious pattern about my little house. . . .
'Here am I', the Stranger said,

But I was still staring up at the buzzards
From my faithless furrow:
Which of them would tilt and drop for me,
Shadow upon shadow,

Shadow of a death upon shadow of a life
Shadowed by an eternity? . . .
'Here am I', said the gentle Stranger,
But more impatiently;

Then his grave hand prisoned my hand
And his blazing eyes captured mine
Whilst the Shadow came falling, falling,
True as a dropped stone,

Shadow of Death upon shadow of Life
In the shadow of all Eternity. . . .
'Now', challenged the Stranger,
'Dare to name *me*!'

Still So Far Away

The frost-coloured sunshine,
The stone-coloured shade,
Touch with lightest fingertips
This March day,

And shining rods stand everywhere,
And no shadow-tree
But is as delicately sure
As its reality;

And, on the ridge, the fledging copse
Stretches gentle line,
Bird-brown, feather-soft,
To brush the sky.

This day, so like a sleeping child,
Seems scarce to draw a breath,
But in such shining stillness smiles
As might grace the newborn dead. . . .

Over such beauty, Whose fond spell
Prevails? Does it reflect
(Oh, still so far away, I cannot tell!)
More nearly Life, or Death?

Anniversary

Does it make any difference that this is the very day,
Even, perhaps, the hour?
And my eyes regard now such things as you looked on last:
Bright-head, stiff-soldier sweet-williams; and that great
    bush
Starlit with yellow flower.

And the shallow pink roses,
Green-arched over the shed,
Softly loose now their petals on the hot roof,
Softly relinquish life to the wind's rough handling –
Just as when first you were dead.

Does it make any difference if this honey sweetness
Blown from the tangled wall
Were almost the last of your sensual impressions –
And the off-and-on hum of the single-minded bees
Were the last of all?

How can there be a day chosen for remembering?
For me, every day of the year, every night,
Brings back the gaiety, the lightfoot grace
Of your brittle strength; and your profound suffering
Breaks you again before my tortured sight;
And again I stare baffled at that smiling face
After you have made your escape, unseen. . . .
For I cannot tell what such smiling peace may mean.

The Stone Angel and the Stone Man
(1958)

The Stone Angel and the Stone Man

Was it for this that the stone was born?
Ninety years: then this autumn day;
And I, a stranger, trespass here,
Questioning my soul's questioner.
The years must have worked a secret way
With the flesh long before they'd candidly worn

The angel's face to this moron mask,
Blurred and blunted, grimed, and mapped
By spider-travel and industry.
For this that the stone was born? I ask.
Ludicrous, crude! Stone must be shaped
By indwelling power, a soul's history.

Yet dared I mock this traffic-direction
Gesture of petrified love, nineteen
Forgotten years would bow my head
Though my tears all burn for the Stone Man,*
Burn dry, unfallen, uncomforted.
Does God fulfil hopes by contradiction?

Dead at nineteen. Her sprig of death
May have rooted, watered by her own tears,
Grown tall, tall as an archangel,
And for the vagrant eyes of those still left
Unblinded, may have blossomed in the meadow of the stars.
O forgive us as we forgive the Stone Angel!

But the Stone Man lies across our path
Today, nor gives nor asks our forgiveness,
Being of our time; our brother annihilates

* In *The Listener* of 18 October 1956, there appeared a
photograph of a man's petrified body recently discovered at
Pompeii, lying 'as he fell' in A.D. 79.

Nearly two thousand years with this last breath
Whose agony and terror we now witness.
They have photographed the moment when Life meets

Death; for the moment never ended
And now is shared between us and the Stone Man
Who was running from terror into terror. He sprawls
As he fell. He is true: the impossible is demanded,
And the ultimate effort soars to superhuman
Heights of intensity. And falls.

For this, truly stone came to birth
And lives. Our clear choice is stated:
Stone Angel, cliché of hope;
Stone Man, in hopeless truth.
Terror and despair surpassing the limited
Capacity of mortal flesh, leap

To no fame, are neither mourned nor remembered; but
        immortal.
Anguish has no end; itself completes, makes perfect
The incomplete. Christ hangs crucified
And crying to God. This alone is real
For our time, for life, for death:
Christ and the Stone Man have not died.

And yet – the Angel is petrified love;
A lifelong reminder of love to those bereft
Whose unbearable first holiness of grief
Made thankful way for an intruder; into the grave
They had dropped their flower of love; they left
It to a mercy from thought of which men crave relief.

The yellow woods darken. The day
Is in its second youth, the dawn of night.
And I am astounded by an unheralded miracle –
Or did I miss some foretelling, in that sheepdog-grey
And quiet sky, of this glory of light? –
From south to north the western wall
Of the universe has dissolved away at a breath
Unnoticed by fretted flesh or stone!
Nothing now between us and the World of Light!
But saffron, rose, and amethyst, spread
The shadows of Light towards that sapphire-green
Clear lake, on the verge of night. . . .

O word that was not made Flesh,
The soul instantly recognizes your Voice,
And, dumb in its body of death,
Hears the homing centuries rejoice.

Between Snowfalls

Look, this is the place. The end.
The footprints come this far.
Then nothing.
It isn't possible, we both know
That. But who's the liar? The snow
Can't bear false witness.
But snow melts in time;
Let's mark the place somehow,
And come back, and maybe find
The clue we're after.

For how can we exist not knowing
Anything but that a small fourfoot,
A fellow
About whose identity we're still arguing,
Climbed this steep field,
Alone, firmly, without hesitation,
For some purpose, recently,
The snow having stopped at perfection;
And then – almost on the level –
Simply came to an end?

No fur, no blood, no ruffle
Of violence on the blameless snow.
Nothing.
The only spoiling ourselves have made,
Mess rather than pattern, but we understand
The necessity of human guilt;
That's an old trouble. Now we're engaged
On something quite new. May the snow
Melt in our time! Already light
Most gently flows;

Kindly, with slow gentleness
Stroking the deathly land;
But these are those
Who kiss the dead. Neither sound
Nor movement betray the perfection

Of this world of death we have found
Together, standing where a traveller
Ascended, perhaps, into heaven,
Or, perhaps, descended into hell
From a given point.

We ought to know, my dear.
By joining hands, and observing
The unimaginable truth
In the crystal of one another's eyes,
We ought promptly to be be able to uncover
All mysteries. We had a brother
We never saw and he has gone
Leaving an unreadable message
In a dead world blameless
Before God.

The kind light's stroking
Hand falls limp.
Do you think
This snow will melt in our time?
Do you? And shadows return
To those hard, deserted, trees?
This is a strange place, where we stand.
Perhaps we had better get back home
Quickly, and alter our prayers
By firelight.

Asking not for this snow to melt
In our time or any other,
But for a new fall,
Heavy and endless, to undo
The harm we have done, and to obliterate
The evidence we shall never forget
Nor ever find courage to remember.
Turn us now to the black north.
Look! Our redemption waiting
To fall.

A Burial

So I bury this dead mole whose trust was not in earth.
The loose little bag for shapely life is worth
A blessing, I think; but who am I to commend
Into the Creator's joyful waiting hand
This completed creature who never lost
His life's holy ghost?

The time has gone, for me, when a footfall would have
     been heard.
A lifetime passed in listening. Yet I never feared
That the end might come before the step, the knock,
The figure on my threshold dazzling black
Against some low light,
Forestalling forever the night.

A true listener, I, without fear, without hope.
Listening by nature, mind and body taking shape
Accordingly; true as mole-minds;
And as the way of this fur and of these shovel-hands
And of this strong snout, which fulfil
The deep sculptor's skill.

But the time has passed, now. Both Hope and Fear
Offer perpetual companionship in place of that pure,
Unquestioned, unregarded, sureness. But craving
Their difficult pardons, stubbornly, though without
     moving
For an instant either stone,
I beg the truce of being alone.

Methodically Glancing Through a Finished Diary

The first day of the first month
One came over the sea,
Skilled with the waves as a friend of Christ,
Leaping from rolling crest to crest –
'Here,' I cried, 'comes the Holy Ghost!'
For so it seemed to me.

The second day of the second month
Rain pranced in the air,
Mist folded the strangled sea
Into land and sky, the sycamore tree
Gleamed like a snake. Suddenly
My life soared in prayer.

The third day of the third month
Tall rods of light
Shone wherever I turned my eyes,
The sea practised innocent ways,
Pigeons of sky in the woodland trees
Wooed a child's sight.

On the fourth day of the fourth month
Angels took the sky,
God entered the bread and wine –
Light as flame the infant green,
Bright as laughter fell the rain,
The sun sprang high.

The fifth day of the fifth month
Was dark almost as night,
Still leaves and silent flowers
Propped the darkness, closing doors
Cut away the living hours.
For what did the soul wait?

The sixth day of the sixth month
Woodlarks had climbed the night,
No footprint stained the grass,
Lupins sentried the window glass,
The battering soul could nowhere pass.
'Which is the way out?'

The seventh day of the seventh month
Flew over my head
In the loosened hand of pain I lay
Hearing the wing-beats of the day
And silvery sunny children at play.
Comparing peace with the dead.

On the eighth day of the eighth month
Lazarus wavered forth
Trembling, brilliant-eyed, whilst love
Quick-coursed the rivers of the blood
And straight from the beamy Man Above
Dived angels of the Lord.

Between the ninth day of the ninth month
And the tenth of the tenth
Stretched a rainbow span, apart
From alpha-omega of the Janus heart,
And the crying finish of the flying start,
And the accurate shadow's length.

The eleventh day of the eleventh month
When the young dead returned
Was there none to wait in the altered light?
None to meet them at the gate
With half-hearing, with half-sight,
While the old fires burned?

On the twelfth day of the twelfth month
Death came over the sea.
Blood poured from the wounded sun
To make his path, the Holy One,
Christ's Ghostly Lover; to shun
Whose courtship dooms to celibacy.
Or so it seemed to me.

So it seems to me.

The House

Listen, children, to a fairy tale
About a house that vanished; vanished for a long while
And was found again – where, do you think?
Under the mountain? On the canyon's brink?
In the huge dim room at the bottom of the sea?
No, but the losers searched persistently
In all such places, by the light of sun,
Moon, stars. And still, when light was done
With forever, seemingly, searched the dangerous night,
Long after they had forgotten for what they sought.

Yes, children, this is a fairy tale.
For the fact is that although the house was real
Enough, the story is too pretty to be true,
As I shall tell it. Otherwise you,
Who are not yet losers, as far as I know,
Might begin weighing this Yes, that No;
Soon, what would be left to remind me of a house
Once known by heart, your way, in grace?
And where could I point to proof, irrefutable evidence
That loss is evitable; substitution stuff and nonsense?

For what is the use of finding again the lost,
Recognizing with delight and a storming passion of
        relief,
Whilst yourself changed beyond recognition, a ghost
And a poor specimen at that? There's grief and grief:
Time may be stronger than the one, I have heard; but
        one
Feeds on the heart until, suddenly,
After years, the structure collapses, from within.
How expect recognition? Reassembled, woodenly
Hobbles the once-lithe: tarnished, slow
And awkward, the sword of laughter makes show.

And so I shall not tell the tale that way,
But the fairy way, which after all may,
Once given, and received by grave eyes,
Be stripped of the label Sparkling Lies
And shown as more true than Sober Truth,
Wiser than sophistry, more faithful than Death
To's true-love Life:
                          the house vanished
One corn-yellow day. The dead banished
Soon the dreamers from hope's curious kingdom,
And quite soon those dreamers forgot their dream.
And yet, the house was found again, unaltered,
Calm, on some other corn-yellow day
In the children's month. And all who belonged entered
Without fuss, making for their places so naturally
That wonder was still-born as to how they had come
Ever to forget that they could always go home.

Convalescence

Yesterday, as far as the broken foxglove;
Today, on to the glittering in the hedge;
Tomorrow, right to the first tree
Of the wood in the valley –
Yesterday, as far as the broken foxglove;
Today, to this glittering tin in the hedge;
Tomorrow, right to the first tree
Of the wood in the valley –

And after that? After that the day will come
When I shall go on and on and on, my lost home
Found in my heart; I, a king bearing his kingdom
Within; never again to turn, never to retrace,
Never to pass any more through the same shadow twice;
Free and light as the dying, in Time; as the dead, in Space.

But I must turn here today.
Turn and go back, as yesterday,
And tomorrow, treading the same way
With everything changed, the freshness gone,
The dripping arch cold, its green
Bright slime dangerous, all vain
The blazing glory of the path at the foot
Of the golden embankment, where my steps obliterate
Outgoing footprints and outgoing thought.

'Did you go too far? Lie down
A while.' 'Has walking brought on the pain?'
'I'll put your tea by the bed and turn
Your bath on early, so rest until then.'
A patient; cared for, protected; love
So passionless and scatheless learning to receive.

Today right up to that glittering tin in the hedge
Though yesterday only with effort as far as the broken
    foxglove
Tomorrow tomorrow to the shadow cast by the first tree
Of the wood in the valley
And soon after that soon soon the day will come
When I shall go on and on and on my found home
Held in my heart.
            A child again? Too sure, too tireless;
And friends with death.

Your Guess Is As Good As Mine

It occurs to me that in darkness Soul goes well,
Leaping like a firefish,
Diving like a star; crammed full
Of godly artifice.

But that Body stumbles whenever left without light,
Mind stammers,
Until each, becoming aware of the other's plight
And heeding rumours

Of devilry, crumbles with fear, and betrays
His onetime friend
In a crazy cracking hope to save
The beginning from the end.

Whilst all the time Soul speeds on through the
    darkness,
Firefish, star.
To forget those inadequate companions? I'd guess,
Just gently to remember.

Snow

As I stood at my threshold
Watching the shadowless snow,
Mind spoke to body
In that voice the dying know:
'See the hill slung with pawprints!
Follow where they lead,
That life and life may celebrate
Death, at the snow's speed.'

Follow such feather-foot guidance
Towards the waiting sky?
Dead white under dead dark
The silent earth might lie
Yet my heart could light no candle,
Nor cry to the Mother of God,
But let the dead rest on Death's breast
And tread where the living had trod.

Over the crest the footprints
Ended. The sky held
Its peace. Some rich berries
Of blood laced the field.

As I stand at my threshold
Watching the shadowless snow,
Mind grieves for body
With that grief the dying know.

Before the Light Fades

Before the light fades
Someone should be found to explain
With sufficient wisdom and patience
Everything I have seen.

And before owl and moth
Shock by remembered flight
The deep, tombed, silence
Of the world of night,

There should appear some linguist
Hot-blooded as a bird,
To translate with a single sentence
Everything I have heard.

Then darkness
Might prove home,
And eternal silence
The kingdom come.

It Is Not Likely Now

It is not likely now.
God's lion crouches low in jeopardy;
It is not likely that a step should sound
So late. Blame all on memory,
The tireless trickster who knows every path,
The way of every latch, mimics a pose in a chair
Truly to life, that the sad stranger Death
Stands back, awkward, and unfamiliar.

It is less likely now.
A great fleet jewels the sky tonight,
Ships silver-lamped, and green, yellow,
And ruby; and the whole vast sea of midnight
Theirs. Who that could ride with that fleet would return
Here? I would not. I would ride and ride forever,
My deep light brilliant on the dark ocean,
A sign for my harmless and forgotten lover.

It will soon be dawn now,
For the little wolf-wind whimpers like a child.
Why should I wait and wait who have never found,
Never, anything by waiting? And have won the right
To that flawless freedom which is death-in-life: freedom
Never to be welcomed nor to welcome; never to turn the head
And wave; nor for the mind to hare leaping home
In advance. The only treasure of the living dead.

Nothing is likely now.
An angel has flung back the futile stone
And lion-Christ, God's darling, proud
And triumphing, strides freshly forth, done
Perhaps with death forever. Day without end?
Night is the flower of day; and at evening they come home
Who are coming. Count them on the thumb of one hand.
Before you have finished, again evening will have come.

A Clear Shell

Then fire burned my body to a clear shell.
Though whether the fanning tempest blew from hell
Or heaven I could not, cannot, tell –
Who have no sense
Left for so nice a difference.

But I learned the essential function of extreme pain –
Of liquid fire pouring again and again
And again through the horrified body: such pain
Makes wholly innocent.
Therefore am I impenitent

Today. Today ask no forgiveness,
Having nothing to be forgiven. And my soul, no less
House-proud than at the beginning, shows Death
Smilingly over the place,
Trusting this new face.

Hospital Car

Impossible to forget sliding down, down
Into the starry pool of that little lighted town
Whilst black fog towered on the moorland side;
Nor the curious way in which I was forced to interpret
The gesture of the accustomed hand closing his gate –
A month before he died.

I had not knowledge of him, nor he of me.
We had travelled together without speech, weary
In our separate fashions; parted with a word and a smile.
Then how could hands' quiet ordinary gesture
In the March dusk have made me so blindingly sure
Of what tongue would never tell?

Chronic Ward

The copper-beeches that have witnessed all
The fury of my caged and battering soul
Droop silent,
Droop indifferent,
Plum-coloured in the small dull
Rain, and most suitably mournful
For the frequent hearse, for the credulous, careful,
Invalid watchers at the window who have been told:
'Copper-beeches are beautiful.
And you are now too old
For concern about anything except Food and Sleep:
Food and food, sleep and sleep.
Remember also to worship caution
And hallow resignation,
That, by little insipid doses, less
And less may remain of the final draught of death.'

But I, alone with my death, have seen Death
As the flower of Life, where Light is the flower of Darkness.
And have known we were born to cherish that flower from its
      start —
Tend, nourish, plead its deliverance from evil,
That it open clear into angel perfection at last,
The fulfilment, the glory, the cause and the purpose of all.

Yellow Evening

To hide the things that I had seen
From my spirit, before I slept
I died into a corpse's dream
Wherein none wept,

None laughed; nor ever did hope or fear
Drink from the heart's cup;
Nor did the hemlock of despair
Grow tall on the grave of love.

To hide the things that I had seen
From my spirit, I faithless died,
Breaking trust with the lover Sun,
The crucified.

So let him hang from the bright-flowered tree
Against the lemon sky.
Those angels of the glittering sea
May show more pity than I.

But now, in the straight and yellow light,
My soul between hedges of flame
Runs, facing the door of night
That opens for its shame.

A Wounded House

Waiting in the silent house,
Not knowing if anyone is there
(I found the door unbolted, the fire burning),
Violently I am made aware
Of the passionate heart's one sureness: loss.
But cower back from the moment's warning,

For who lit this fire
Should justly see it die;
Whose breath in this still room yet floating
Mingles inseparably with mine,
Should soon return – even hides somewhere here,
Watches, listens, mimics my waiting. –

But I wait in a wounded house.
And now, acute in my rôle of lover,
Sense the life here flowing away, flowing
And never to be staunched, yet never
To bleed itself dry until the perfection of loss
Triumph in our love's own dying.

The Proof

As I walk walk free in heaven
Kicking the dusty stars
I fancy the passing angels smile
To witness my capering airs.
O, I fancy their glances tender,
Astonished, envious. –
Though I can never be sure because
My eyes were burnt out in hell.

Still, I caper about in heaven
Young as the day I began,
And when the Sun's broad palm I feel
On my shoulder, 'The heart of a man',
I marvel, 'is no way lesser
To God's love than a blade of grass!' –
But I can never be sure because
My heart burned out in hell.

If I lie down to rest in this heaven
At last, blind and alone
And danced to a spent standstill,
Need I know God's dream from my own?
The Soul flowers for ever,
Droops not nor withers the Rose. –
O, of this I am sure, am sure, because
My soul burns unquenched in hell.

The Exile

The fool said to the animals:
'You are merely my chattels,
With one lesson to learn –
That what happens to you is not your concern
But mine; for a just God has set
You on earth for my profit.'

The animals answered the fool
Nothing at all,
But for a single moment
Turned on him their wild, true, innocent
Eyes, where an Angel of the Lord
Holds Eden's flaming sword.

Moth at a Window

Moth at a window-pane frantic for glory
With jewel-red eyes cannot rest cannot tire
Nor question the Power over the glory
That turns the lamp lower, lower, lower.

Moth at a window cannot premeditate
Coolness of loss, the dark nature of peace;
As lover, poet, saint, must dedicate
(O the garnet eyes in the phantom face!)

Instinct, will, desire, vocation,
To a perfect clear integrity
Of ruthless thoughtless selfless ambition
Luminous with passion's necessity.

Sad that the Power over the glory
Should turn the lamp lower. Soon it will fade,
Bringing the commonplace end to the story.

Or the lighted window may be thrown wide.

A Few Moments in Late Evening

The fire in my rich bones
Is the fire in the glittering tree.
Ah, how the diamond river flows!
How light flows through the trembling tree!

The black leaves lift, tremble,
Thrust by the flowing flame;
Glittering as water, what shall it kindle
What quench, this Flame?

Survivor

Suddenly my Lord the Sun
Lifting cloud-coffin lid
Glares down the moorland road.
I had thought his day done,

Had thought his fleets of the sky
Soon drowned in fathomless night,
And that never again I
Need endure his persuasion of Light.

Yet now must I stand, turn
Full-face to the violent west,
Whilst the bones of my body burn
And flame is my soul's breath,

And my heart, a gleaming pool
Brim-full of the luminous sky,
Still still still
Lives, though my Lord die.

The Stuttering Water and Other Poems

(1970)

The Stuttering Water

Always, across the orchard the stuttering water pleaded.

On that August Sunday afternoon
In nineteen-forty-three
I looked down from my window
At the sailor looking up at me,
In so deep hidden a place
Most unexpectedly.

'I thought the old place empty
'Or surely I'd not have come.'
Underbreath, *It soon would have been*, I said.
Aloud, 'I know your name.
'You're Larry who ran away to sea.
'This was your home.'

Only the flickering of a grin.
'Never once been back.
'Thought I'd like just to take a look round
'So I loaned me a bike.
'D'you mind?' 'Sailor, why should I mind?' –
So long as you're gone quick.

Not been back in ten years.
Then why today for the surprise?
Breaking into my nick of time
With your carved face, and your eyes'
Blank windows, and your voice
Quiet as the summer sea's.

Though you answer no questions, sailor,
You can't hide from me why you've come
Bicycling all the way from Devonport
For one glimpse of your only home.
It's because you're sailing tomorrow
And know it's the last time.

I've seen others look as you look.
They've come, gone, are past.
Everyone guessed their secret
(Except those to whom it meant most).
Nobody guesses my secret, Larry,
That's mine, first and last.

Larry, wild Larry,
Of whom they still find plenty to tell
Up there in the village, recalling
The freaks of the boy's wild will
And how at fourteen it ran him off to sea.
'Cure?' they say. 'Or kill?'

Did it cure you, Larry?
Had your mother no heart to break?
Did it kill you, Larry,
That you never once came back?
No parents, no brothers here now,
And Larry's come back.

And he's come at the wrong time, sailor,
In the wrong nick of time.
And asking and answering no questions,
As if he thought this still his home,
His was-is-now ever-shall-be
And only home.

If I'd asked fewer questions, sailor,
On fewer lies I'd have fed,
Concerning life-in-death and death-in-life;
The beauty of the dead;
Glitter and gold; the durable nature of fire;
Stones and bread.

Had I been speaking? Thinking?
Had time passed? Stayed still?
The carved face had not altered.
Must both together breathe farewell
To this place? Each in separate silence
Coin the same parable?

For still across the orchard
The stuttering water pleaded.
Though with whom? And which attendant
Accurately heeded?
Or was, for that curious once, our world
Undivided?

*   *   *

When I watched the sailor swinging
Loose and long and light
Away over the water meadow
Where the stream sprawled wide and flat,
It was pretty to see how the silvery spray
Made a dancing frill for each foot.

Bent-head, shoe-contemplative,
Larry no-ears no-eyes,
You've a shadow now cavorting
On the lemon-gold hillside,
For the sun's shattered the rim of the burrows
To the lofty buzzard's cries.

Swerve at the hedge, up on the hillside –
You'll have left the bike at the top gate –
Pulled by a shadow, or the shadow of a shadow,
May Larry not even wait
For a single glance back at his home in the valley
Where the stream runs deep and straight?

My angry mocking ceased. Larry had gone.
Thief of my power to die.
Cancellor of the appointment fixed between sunset
And sunset, in my nick of time.
Broken that nick. My chains reforged.
My dark newly tortured by light.

Yet still across the orchard
The stuttering water pleaded.
Have I not listened? Name of Christ!
Have I not heeded?
Your pleading maddened the dare-devil boy
And by whom then was the guide guided?

My raging spirit fell to earth,
Fallen fire died down.
Rose the gentle phoenix, prayer,
For Larry who had gone.
That he might turn and lift his eyes
Southward to Caradon.

Let him forget the water's voice,
Lift his eyes where no help comes
Save peace that is not his or mine
Until ashes be fanned to flames
By the same breath which was the breath
Of our first and lasting times.

*   *   *

Up in the village shop next day
I found them all standing round
Talking of Larry and his death . . .
I heard, my spirit swooned.
Half-conscious, wholly sentient,
I stood my listening ground.

The morning of the day before
(They were saying) there'd been an explosion
In the engine-room of Larry's ship.
Larry had been thrown
Against a boiler, with such force
As broke him. How was it known?

Oh, someone's cousin's friend
Had met someone else that night
Who'd been in a pub with Larry's pal
Whom he'd told about hiring a bike
And meaning to ride, that afternoon
Into Cornwall. At sunset he died.

It's not true, I said, speaking no word.
I tell you, it's no sense at all.
Larry went bounding up the hillside
As yesterday's sun broke that wall
At the end of the burrows. I watched him go,
And his shadow went as well.

'Shadow of a shadow'. Who said these words?
And why should Jan, the little hunchback,
At my side have tilted on his heels
And with splendid head pressed back
Be looking up from his hill-watching peat-coloured
    eyes
At my face and its naked shock?

Still, across the distance the stuttering water pleads.

In Place

In clear gilt sunlight
At one-seventeen p.m.
On this twenty-fifth day of April
Rests this lizard

On this primrose leaf.
Elect for the poised and almost weightless weight
This particular lolled tongue of a leaf in the hedge

Enables perfection.
A young male lizard:
New to this aspect of the world,
For scarcely had he opened to the sliding autumn
Before his ordered closing in dark's depth.
Now he gleams shell-like, lids drawn
In the beatific face, jutted elbows
And firmly spread fingers propping
The raised torso of this infant son
Of the god who pulses featherweight as yet
Through the very young warmth and brightness
Of the upspringing world.

Here, then, is executed the perfection of a design
Brought from and through all Time
Into this moment – into this timed moment
Out of all Time past and all to come –
Into this accurate timed moment which being perfect
Could not be out of place
In Eternity.

All in the Day's Work

NOTE

During the 1960's Frances Bellerby collected poems
for a volume with this title, but it was never
published. Charles Causley included a number of
these in his *Selected Poems* (Enitharmon, 1970).
Others were revised and later appeared in *The
First-Known* in 1975. Since many of these poems
underwent extensive revision during ten or more
years, it is difficult to say just when the final versions
were written. In one case I have preferred an earlier
version in manuscript to a published one, but I give
both versions.

A.S.

Ends Meet

My grandmother came down the steps into the garden.
She shone in the gauzy air.
She said: 'There's an old woman at the gate –
See what she wants, my dear.'

My grandmother's eyes were blue like the damsels
Darting and swerving above the stream,
Or like the kingfisher arrow shot into darkness
Through the archway's dripping gleam.

My grandmother's hair was silver as sunlight.
The sun had been poured right over her, I saw,
And ran down her dress and spread a pool for her shadow
To float in. And she would live for evermore.

There was nobody at the gate when I got there.
Not even a shadow hauling along the road,
Nor my yellow snail delicate under the ivy,
Nor my sheltering cold-stone toad.

But the sunflowers aloft were calm. They'd seen no one.
They were sucking light, for ever and a day.
So I busied myself with going away unheeded
And with having nothing to say.

No comment, nothing to tell, or to think,
Whilst the day followed the homing sun.
There was no old woman at my grandmother's gate.

And there isn't at mine.

Slipped Useless Away

With pen cut from moon's horn
And dipped in blood of sun
I wrote first on the surface of the sea.
Was that so ill-done?

Then, paring my spread wits
To lightning point of judgement,
I slashed the second poem on the wind.
Call that a slight achievement?

The third on sand, fourth on snow,
Took ordained shape.
Fifth flowed out onto a rainbow
With neither pause nor slip.

Sixthly, dived that streaming star
From heaven's tall peak,
Blazoned in sizzling letters of fire
With words I was born to speak.

Now may the seventh leave me alone
To the dark grace of the dead
And cool mortal kindness of this stone,
My daily bread.

Regrettable Return

'D'you mean she's lost?
It was under this hill
That she lived, the woman
We children knew so well.

'Ages ago we all
Scattered or died –
But I'll find her without anyone
To go at my side.'

And I've not the least need
To go far to look,
For nightfall and moonrise
Always brought her back. . . .

I remember this looped track
Under the trees.
Where it passes the well
Any accustomed gaze

Homeward flies. . . .
But how the windows stare!

Christ! What's now
The welcome here?

There

It was there she lived, there,
Under that hill,
The solitary woman
I knew well.

If the children who learnt her ways
Have scattered or died
Someone must be left
To be my guide,

Someone left to tell me
Where to look,
Or if nightfolk and moonrise
May bring her back

Down the rough old road
Under the trees
Past the well in the wall
Her homing gaze

Flying from door's blank
To windows' stare,
Expecting God-Knows-What
Welcome there.

Contemporary

Someone told me this road led to a star
and a stable, but I'll get nowhere tonight,
with the way the velvet snow
slipshods my feet.

I'd better search about for a resting-place
which I can pretend is a half-way house to home.
'Hey! Who has a lair?
My time is come!'

Where other animals have sheltered, burdened as I,
and bowing to earth have brought forth
(I like old words),
let me deliver my lord.

But it must be a place from which no track shall ever lead
and in a dark forever unscarred by light
and though my coming will wound the snow
it must heal, immaculate.

And I will change the appointed end, Fox, owl,
hare, shall guide me through this maze of danger;
for I have seen too many crucified.
And none a stranger.

 This is an earlier version of *Regrettable Return* (printed on p. 121)

That Risen Sun

Do you by chance remember
The sea suddenly puckering
As if to sneeze, or yawn?
And how we actually saw the slender wind, greenish silver,
Flowing out of the south-east towards which we started to
     swim,
With the day in our faces? We could afford to let the gulls
     Ha-ha,
Our darkness being over, our fears having proved flimsy as
     shell.
Innocence and experience in our salt veins sang duet:
'This risen sun shall never set.'

1915

Never mourn the deathless dead
Whilst meteors glide across the sky
Between the crowding stars. Though there cried
A murdered childhood worlds away
In August nights for none to hear,
Attend now Altair's trumpet-note of fire.

Sight and hearing being one
The Plough makes music as much as light.
Sharp from the anvil of the night
A struck spark shouts, falls dumb.
You saw? You heard?
Time does not keep, nor eternity break, this Word.

Grieve no more for the agony of the child.
She'd have brooked no lighter grief
Who watched through tears the blackest field
Against the silverest sky. No thief
Was pure to snatch such treasure
From the unmeasured heart that's made your measure.

The Possible Prayer

Fox flares not for her
Nor shall light bloom in tree
For penniless eyes to see.
But, whilst the oaks like shadows
Lie on the steep meadows
Under dovewing cloud,
Is time to prepare the shroud
For her doomed March fear
To the tune of this possible prayer:

That fear drop dead before oncoming death.
Pain be grounded under Christ's heel
Whilst still the holy communicant breath
Tastes bread and wine. That some seashell
From the home shore to be held to the ear
Now now and by a recognized hand
The music overlapping the senses' end
As the fall of that living wave on the shore
Overlapped and annulled its following death.

The Disappointment of Robert Clayton
(. . . if his son ask bread, will he give him a stone?)

Not mother's curved love
Nor father's tall despair
Not yellow August sun
Nor the heady taste of air

Weakened Robert Clayton
Who left others to grieve
And stern-jawed with determination
Tearless took his leave.

But tears of man and woman
Flowing together made
Stone life for Robert Clayton
For whom there was no bread,

And stone kingdom come
Robert's infant face
Set   determined   grim
Caught its defiant peace.

*   *   *

Set against life? Or death?
She alone might say
To whom the unpractised breath
Gave secrets away.

In nine months of sharing
An impregnable and dedicated house
Two had worked preparing
One's dwelling-place;

Did none of it please, then?
Surely life the illuminator
Kindled for Robert Clayton
Sixty candles to an hour –

Only for death to dash them out
Before his quickening affronted eyes
With a 'Not for you, and not
For your greedy mind's surmise.'

*   *   *

He won, though, Robert Clayton.
See the jutted lip's twist.
Contemptuous, that. 'Get on
Bully Death, since you must.

'My mother's love I'll quit,
My father's joy deface;
Of air, let a single sip,
Of sun, one shaft, suffice.

'Others than Robert Clayton
For him may choose to cry.
Jutting my jaw with determination
I'll tearless die.'

*   *   *

Stone kingdom come
Robert's infant face
Set   determined   grim
Holds it defiant peace.

A photograph in *The Listener*, 5 December 1957, showed
the remarkable effigy in St. Giles' Church, Ickenham,
Middlesex, of Robert Clayton 'who dyed 16th of August
1665 within a few howres after his birth.'

Remember Without Pity

At the instant when hare looks up and eagle looks down
The earth's heart halts it gnomic tune
And all stand waiting for the softfoot priest
Wordless to lift the chalice, break the host.

Then remember without pity how the same hare flowed
Up the steep ploughland, swifter than the March light
And itself firelit by some flame of lively God,
Into clearness to leap beyond clutch of your beggarly sight.

And never forget that four are included in the dream.
Priest, hare, eagle, and the audience to give
Ear to the seasoned ballad of a fourfold doom
And a fourfold redemption and union for ever in love.

FROM

The First-Known and Other Poems

(1975)

The Heron

But that was not the whole story.
     The night fallen away, you could stand up to your
         ankles
     In platters of frozen snow on the flooded grass
     And stare, and curse a supposed god of some kind,
     And at last touch, as guiltily as though to break faith
     With an absent friend : spreading the rounded wing
     Tenderly grey as an archangel cygnet might be,
     Springing it again, inappropriately elastic for death,
     Lifting the flopped and folded neck, empty
     Rubber, absurd to imagine as support for that hard
     Weight of head and great sword bill
     (Stone dangling in a sling; hanged man
     At rope's end jerking, aping horridly
     The Spirit that had informed him). The long powerful
         legs
     Might still be life's; but cramped claws, famined
     Body, that shocking useless neck, acknowledge
     Death; and the dulled eye's a mere object
     For examination in itself, no more a window
     For the claustrophobic ghost, proved not viable.

But that was not the whole story.
     Above the steep orchard where three ewes and their
         lambs
     Had been brought to their crumb of mercy, the wind
         raved,
     The murderer, and nothing had breath but for
         enduring for enduring,
     Whilst the snow had erased meanings uncontained by
         death
     And by the dark north leaning heavily on the land
     And on the horrified heart, bestowing griefless despair.

Neither was that the whole story.
     In the deep derelict garden by the stream, the living
     Screamed for life, wings battled beaks
     Claws tore ransacked the ruined snow
     The rotted leaves the clumped and clammy earth
     To scatter the broken heap of holy apples
     Tipped unconsecrate in the heedless summer's end.
     Attack, devour, tear the heart out of the Word
     Made Flesh! This they do in remembrance
     Of life, faithfully and never count their dead
     Nor have knowledge of night though night's in
         abeyance only.
     Soon, even these wings will obey the dark
     And the clamour will drop for death to go his rounds.
     Which will die, head-first in hollows
     Amongst roots? Fall from branches and ledges, heads
     Still under wings? Diminished and stiff travesties
     To be spurned by the dawn, and mocking the overnight
         prayer
     'Send them an angel, send them an angel, send! –'

But that was not the whole story.
     No one in senses prays to be answered. Praying
     Must make its own answer. Find a place where the
         echo's
     Clear and true, that's all. 'Send them an an-gel!'
     'An-gel'. – What more could you want? The Word of
         God
     Fleshed before your very eyes? There may be a moment
     For that also, when lower-case time's
     Done, and capital Time that cannot be wasted,
     Nor killed even humanely, becomes visible, tangible,
     Closer than lover, and turns out to have been always
         simply

That principle of Love, the stream of eternal water
Flowing through the caves with imperious thudding
    and thunder
But soundless in the open. Though what can the
    principle of Love
Be about in any disguise but that of grief? Whose tears
Fall on the dead Heron? Who counts
Each dawn the small dead under the bank?
And leaves them lying. The death-mad Fox
May come before the snow. May out-stare death.
May frisk in the buoyant weather when Heron and
    Redwings
Haunt only the haunted, and the living shout
For joy, labour for joy, and it can be seen even by man
That joy is also a disguise of the principle of Love.
Then the minute yellow spider will be watched in the
    grass
Carrying her large blue ball with the care,
Skill, forethought, industry, of her whole being,
Setting it down that she may go ahead to reconnoitre,
Returning to hoist and heave it to the chosen halt
From which she will again reconnoitre, making all safe,
    protected,
For her treasure, her tremendous share of the riches of
    the God
Of Love. Who himself offers no protection,
Guides to no sanctuary, but anneals tenderness
To a passion, making each individual life a supreme
Unique dedication, and each individual death
A tragedy to purge with pity and terror the innocent
Children of men with their bloodstained hands.
                          The principle
Clears, and the half-hoping heart must cry
'Send them an angel! Send!' but who hears?

The echo? –
              Once there was a childhood orchard. In a
        high
Corner children could call, and always be answered
Satisfyingly by the clear precise echo, but no
Man or woman ever. It was taken as proof
Positive that each child in turn had definitely
Grown up, when the echo no longer replied.
And naturally before long there was nobody who had
        not climbed
Up to that corner for the last try. The end of the story
Might be the initiation of the first child's first child
And the delightful rediscovery of that barbaric and
        fastidious echo
Good as new : everyone concerned satisfied.
But things seldom happen that way. Still, there's a
        point.
Fool's guess with sporting chance of being right.
Delirium's solution. Seer's incommunicable vision.
Ultimate innocence of experience. Proof positive
As that strict mathematical answer to the problem of
        the universe
Sometimes revealed, in white fire, under dental gas,
And lost by returning consciousness though the fact
        remains,
Laughably, for life : the answer having been actually
        found
And perfectly understood, satisfying as nothing that
        followed
Ever was. Years bring no wisdom
To the once-satisfied except denial of hope, and
        realization
Of the past : if you heard the echo, saw the white
Fire, you know for ever that they exist. What difference

Can it make never to hear or see again?
'*All the difference in the world*'. Speaks the Heron?
Staring down at the dead and thinking of the living
Is cause for tears. All the difference in the world.

If there is an end to the story it comes later.
      When again the moon burns and light flows,
      Grass waves in the wind, and the sleeper hears
      Lucid and sure the echo's answer to prayer
      (Though death fold the Heron in his dream as in the
          world
      He and the Heron knew). Then will the difference
      Vanish as the God of Love transfigures the everlasting
      Dead that they shine with lively light in the flowing
      Time of foregiveness of all winters, when the Vixen
      Dances with her cubs and the Spider's care is great
      And order has burnt up chaos and the world is calm.

First Day Of September

[Token of love and honour for
Patrick Bromby Mace, poet.
Died August 27, 1970]

Walking by this shallow brook,
Desolate for the dead,
By the senses' dispassionate customs
I am befriended.

This appearance of peat-brown water
Slithering under trees
Engages my fancy to account
For light's unaccountable ways.

Those sparklings might be a handful of trinkets
Tossed in some conjuror's game.
These fish-like glittering and flashes
Make havoc of the smooth theme.

Now I see that the overhung water
Is all flicked by strokes
Of rippling silver. But how motionless
The topaz light that glows

Gently, in pieces fallen
Like manna on water and on grass! –
And wafers of the same elucidation
Grace this leafy path.

Leaves. Tawny as Eggars,
As Brimstones yellow.
Autumn? Summer's in the voices
Of the water, whose fellow,

That summer dove, repeats,
Liquid, cool,

Two-and-a-half pleas endlessly;
A servant of ritual.

Yes, nearly un-noticeable
The voices – so slight
A tinkling, a trifling, a plash;
Absorbed and private

As children's talk in bed.
Yet an eavesdropper may feel
The ancient longing for death
As the world and his heart fall still.

Stilled, I look ahead, where the water,
Flattened, loosely spread,
Shines milk-blue and innocent,
By clumps of cress islanded.

I cross. Walk on. This bank
Rises high above the water.
The field on my left's as steep
As a roof. I walk in its gutter.

My sight is suddenly caught –
Down there, through the broken hedge –
By richest blue. The water's
Blue as alkanet!

I clamber down to a gate
Giving on to the stream's bed;
The sprawled water is colourless
And voiceless as the dead.

Beyond there's that shelterless field
Blazing with light . . .
But here's the peace for dazzled day,
To soothe it to its night.

The Dying Of A Child

Not so high as the foxgloves,
Not having sloughed one skin,
He's travelled beyond my furthest reach
To balance on the world's rim.

I fear that the lion sun's
Glare may have been too bright? –
Yet how soon that glare would have failed
Before soft slinking night.

Child, child, child,
Whose peril's mine,
Whose body's my heart's bread,
Blood, its wine –

See the beseeching sun
Pad gently as a pet;
And now floats the buoyant moon
Soothing the nerves of your night.

Falter, for you dare falter –
Being uncluttered, untaught, undaunted –,
Thinking of the emerald fields and the sea
Evermore of you disappointed . . .

       *   *   *

Ah! Save your tears, friends.
He's come, to my pierced side!
In me his tearing hands
Durable shelter have made.

So let Sun raise his head
Shaking the dew from his mane.
Let Moon smile her gliding way
Into sweet brief oblivion,

Whilst through all the emerald fields
And by the miles of swan-white sea
I walk, the fortress of my heart
Secure against eternity.

An Error Corrected

What should I want with bread?
In my curved grip
See this valid stone –
Acorn in cup.

If once, weeping tears of blood
Through the black of a night,
Famished heart pleaded a crumb
Cancel, forget,

Keen God of stone; by whose
Immense perception.
Here, now, this hungry hand
Is filled to perfection.

A Possible Prayer On New Year's Day

To the Light now invisible
Word now inaudible
Truth now unknowable

Pray for the appearance of shadows
Before this New Year's Night.
For shadow trees on the cold null meadows,
Proof of the sun's light.
And pray for each shadow to be delicate and precise
    as its tree,
Now and in memory.

The Death Of The Day

'Lady!' pleaded the beggar,
'Give, give, oh give!
Beautiful you are and rich,
May I not even live?'

But she never heeded,
Gliding on her way,
Never glanced to right or left
In the dying of the day.

'Lady!' cried the beggar,
'Praise be to heaven
For all you've neither looked nor said
And all you have not given!

'Your only jewels now be tears,
Your gold the sun's last flame,
But if treasure you find in the silver night
Praise be to heaven again.'

On on she glided,
Faster she sped
Never flickering a glance
Nor turning her bright head.

Yet when in her eyeballs the risen moon
Glinted, up flew her hands
To cover close those wild eyes.
What is it she defends?

Far ahead the river,
More snow-white than the moon,
Snaked through the silvered valley.
She's gone, gone, gone.

May she, who could not give,
Either hold or take?
What treasure in the valley's trust
Dare one so piteous seek?

'Lady!' shouted the beggar.
'Stay! Come back to me!
You go to desperate peril:
Your saviour – I am he!'

But on on she glided,
Far she sped away,
Never looking to right or left
In the death of the day.

The Angel

'Fear not!' said the Angel,
     appearing in the guise of a shadow
     crossing at the end of the bed
     in the shadowless midnight room
     of the house which had lost its bearings.
     Or so it seemed to the dream-shocked child,
     which comes to the same thing.

'Fear not!' said the Angel,
     appearing in the guise of a pebble
     exactly rounded to the hand
     of the shoe-contemplative wanderer
     by the sleek and voiceless river.
     Or so it seemed to that mournful wanderer,
     which comes to the same thing.

'Fear not!' said the Angel,
     appearing in the guise of a vixen
     dancing twirling in the snow
     in the angle of the orchard hedges
     watched from that window of terror.
     Or so it seemed to the watcher at the window,
     which comes to the same thing.

After that, no angel appeared
     in any guise whatsoever
     to the one so accustomed to guises,
     unless Pain could count as an angel;
     or life's single attainable perfection
     that guiltless companion Despair –
     which might come to the same thing.

Bereaved Child's First Night

I've come to close your door, my handsome, my darling,
I've come to close your door and never come again.
The shadow on the ceiling will not be mine, my darling,
So if you wake in terror cry some other name.

There's first time and last, my handsome, my treasure,
No other time, nothing between.
So whenever the hand of darkness clenches on your candle
Shut your eyes, my darling, and slip back into our dream.

The Sunset Of That Day

Lazarus dare not raise his eyes
above the hooded valley.
Dare not level his weak sight
with that flooded glory.
Death-black on crystal clarity
a coast line there
edges a wide estuary
of primrose water fair
and smiling as though nothing had to die.
Time displaying eternity.

This peace and loveliness
Lazarus cannot share,
nor that most gentle shadowless
further honey-gold shore
detailed there in light:
rock-bound pools, sand,
shallow coves beneath kind
woods which lie deliberate
as gentle beasts at rest,
sun-yellow in that shadowless
light unseen by Lazarus,
death's brief departed guest.

So there'll be no recall
of this first evening of his resurrection
except by touch of grass
cool to the feet – and quickly then
blackbird's loud rattling call.
It will be this and this
that store for Lazarus all
his dazed and trembling bliss,
his charmed and freshened life
brilliant with death, the ratified
lord of his heart still safe,
still uncrucified.

Moon And Tree

Watching this night's yellow moon
Climbing the broken tree
Demands nothing at all of the heart,
Not hate nor love nor pity.

There was a fool mourned the reflection of a star
In some deep-banked pool,
Grieving for light lost, drowned,
Yet briefly visible.

Another prayed for the stricken sun,
Believing he could rise again
Only if strong angels came
To roll back death's stone.

But tears, pity, passion, prayer,
Hate, love, hold no interest for me,
Concentrating on tonight's yellow moon
Climbing the broken tree.

The Valley

Black hills cup the unbreathing deep valley,
enclosing a lake of light from the great moon
such as might minister to the mind's fear and folly.
But it turns away too soon.

Or spanglings of moonlight, scattered flowers of the rooted
    darkness,
reconciling black with the calm intensity of white,
might pacify the mind, its ancient duress
forgiving, to see beyond sight,

And redeemed, innocent, impartial, this once-in-a-lifetime
    fearlessly
perceive eternity manifest, precise, and here —
not shadows and then surmised far reality
but entireness brilliantly clear.

But the heart has the mind in thrall, lost for its own seeking,
shuddering away from the terrible beauty of night —
from the dark for its flower, from the dead for their waking,
from the valley of the shadow for its lake of light.

Dream

To a cry in this night
I have come home.
Through distance and time
fevered I came.

Darkness.
Thudding autumn stream.
Unbreathing house.
But a candle's straight flame!

One lit this candle
whose despair
stirred not a single
cobweb here.

Christ! Could the hand
which lit the flame
touch now my hand
in this dead room! . . .

Someone's here with me
(so still, so still)
whom I cannot see
and dare not call.

Whose was that voice
which cried out, alone
in this sunk house?

Who breathes 'your own'?

Swinging Along The Road

Swinging along the road
between Here and There,
travelling light, being freed
at last from hope and fear,
and the day almost done
and the heart almost cold –
what should I come upon
but a murdered child.

Lying as white as foam
on the flattened wayside grass.
Still, still as stone.
Spread like a little cross.
And blood with shadow matched
making a shadow bed –
though bright were the rivulets I watched
jewel the thirsty road.

Would I had hastened by
with my shuddering
before that torrent of light
from the westering
sun revealed to me
at the start windows of those eyes
where surely none should be –
one I must recognize.

And white though the spun foam lay,
still the stone, the shadow bed,
yet these streaming tears pray
'Christ, let the dead be dead!'
as I run towards the west,
blind in the blazing light,
hot-foot to keep a child's tryst
with endless night.

Winter Solstice and the Christmas Child

In the deep womb of Winter
the darling Child has quickened,
the light, the promise, flickered
and the shadow, the threat.

This tender and profound Winter
is prepared to part now with its darling,
for never may Life be its nursling,
but born of its death.

This riven and bereft Winter
achieving the triumph of its anguish
now drives from the womb the unblemished
Child of the life-giving dead.

The Quarrymen

'Flowers soften sorrow'
the flower-sellers say.
But the quarrymen are silent,
who give their goods away.

Pebbles for the pocket,
millstones for the neck,
milestones for journeys out –
who heeds them on journeys back?

Gravestones for oblivion,
stone hearts for ducks-and-drake,
one quiet stone man for history
to discover, but not to awake.

As for the starving, the desperate,
who hurled their reckless bread
far out to sea in some summer's dawn –
with wilderness stones they're fed.

Then there are the monstrous boulders
with which we block up the tombs
of those whose rest we thus defend –
until some strolling angel comes

Along, and kicks the thing aside,
any sweet night in spring.
Tidied and empty our treasure-house
before the first birds sing!

Not that we tell the quarrymen.
Discouraged, they might shed
their divine responsibility
for this world's daily bread.

On the Third Evening

On the third evening,
coming out of the hillside wood
and for the first time hesitating,
I saw that the hedgeless road
on the one hand leapt up towards the west
to vanish in streaming light,
on the other plunged into a wooded cleft
already deep with night.

Why should I hesitate
who had no way to lose?
For what could it be worthwhile to wait?
Lies had long been my truth.
Moor or valley, what matter? Either would serve
to lead to some sort of end
one who'd uncaringly ceased to search
or wish even to be found.

Yet there I stood,
alerted by sharpest doubt,
at the edge of the voiceless wood,
looking this way, that.
Forsaken, forsaking, a wandering alien had come
on life's imperious last choice.
'Which way', I cried, 'would take me home?' . . .
The universe held its peace.

Strange Return

What am I doing here? – In a place
that seems unknowing, perhaps unknown.
My long journey's sole purposed end
was at last, at last, a return home.
So keen-eyed for landmarks, the map so clear in my mind,
how could I have been misled to this desolate house?

Yet if this were truly a stranger's arrival
would senses know their way about
without mind? Foot's ready for the sloping tread
of the bottom stair. Eye, for the wave in the wall
by that deep window – and further, looking out,
for the orchard's triangle, the tilt of the roof of the shed.

And how do I know the clattering which rain makes on the
       iron
whilst falling soundless on the rotting thatch
of the house? And that up there's the hole where the young
       owls stare
down on summer evenings? Oh, surely I'd watch,
if I stayed here now, things I watched before.
Yet how can the unforgetting be a stranger? Or forgotten?

Still, none has taken my place.
After all, they must have been used to me here. They?
Birds, rats, moles, stoats,
ceiling beams, spider in her cave,
grass, trees, stuttering water, stones . . .
And shadows, playfellows of light in this deep house.

Shadows according to the time of year.
In March, a honeycomb suddenly on that wall.
Only in March. Summer's sun rides
too high for this low room. The full
glorification's by early autumn's westering light
flowing through the tall grasses, from the brink of the moor.

Later, sun's face is withheld.
A secret, behind the towering burrows on the south —
though still shadows move in the mind, the mind's sight
ready to be startled; when all sound
is lost in some roaring gale, or in silence, let
the latch lift and a shadow stand on the threshold . . .

But shadows on the threshold neither answer nor heed
questions, pleadings, flashes of welcome or of fear,
their purpose being only to enter when they belong.
They are too innocent. Why should they care
whose is the heart that beats unfaltering, strong,
through the death that is always Now, and nevermore
        shall be?

The First-Known

I am free to come and go –
That is the bargain I have made.
The door stands wide. Is never closed.
The threshold's worn by me and the dead.

When the wind rages, and the rain,
hurled half-across the impassive room,
streams down my lifted face like tears,
I hear the calling of my name

Tossed in the tempest, here and there,
by that immortal first-known voice
– my friend, my lover, my unseen
gaoler in this hidden place.

One day, one night, one dawn, one dusk,
I will call back, not hesitate,
nor search my memory, heart and mind,
for that dear Name. But still not yet.

Freedom's my chain. Take that and give
truth. Uncloud my hindered eyes,
unstop my ears, that once for all
I see, and hear, and recognize.

Come In Out Of The Night

Come in out of the night,
you who cry my name out there! –
Now the door's wide cannot you see
flowering lamp, capering fire?

Never again until you've come
shall this door be closed by night or day
whilst I have life. And whilst you live,
immortal is my mortal clay.

Over those fields you crying go
as though you had returned to find
a desolate house, deserted, cold,
no gleam of light, no breath, no sound.

And when I call your name, you've gone
weeping your sorrow towards the moor.
Pray for all wanderers! I pray
wandering Christ will meet you there.

The moor must take and give its due.
Then you'll come back. Why do I fear?
Is not the Power that links us two
stronger than fire, more free than air?

But on some night such a storm may rage
as will drive you, helpless, hurled ahead
into this quiet. Here to lie still.
And never know I'm at your side.

The Room

'Child! Child! Come along in!
Old Sun's at downfall,
time you were in bed,
or you'll miss the light on the wall
that you so love.'

'I came in long ago.
I never miss the light on the wall
that I so love.
I never shall.'

Brother and Sister

Would you say that field is the one?
Look, my dear, there's the great
pink chestnut, and the straight path
from iron gate to iron gate –
the old sort, that you wind yourself through.
Yes, that field is the one.

Then the tree's shadow must still make a tent.
What are we so troubled about, the two of us?
There's shelter, freedom, and the whole of time
whilst that slow sun follows its long course,
and in and out of the shadow-tent play,
those deathless children, to our hearts' content.

All Souls' Day

Let's go our old way
by the stream, and kick the leaves
as we always did, to make
the rhythm of breaking waves.

This day draws no breath –
shows no colour anywhere
except for the leaves – in their death
brilliant as never before.

Yellow of Brimstone Butterfly,
brown of Oak Eggar Moth –
you'd say. And I'd be wondering why
a summer never seems lost

if two have been together,
witnessing the variousness of light,
and the same two in lustreless November
enter the year's night . .

The slow-worm stream – how still!
Above that spider's unguarded door,
look – dull pearls . . . Time's full,
brimming, can hold no more.

Next moment (we well know,
my darling, you and I)
what the small day cannot hold
must spill into eternity.

So perhaps we should move cat-soft
meanwhile, and leave everything unsaid,
until no shadow of risk can be left
of disturbing the scatheless dead.

Ah, but you were always leaf-light.
And you so seldom talk
as we go. But there at my side
through the bright leaves you walk.

And yet – touch my hand
that I may be quite without fear,
for it seems as though a mist descends
and the leaves where you walk do not stir . . .

Light

When the sun goes into the wood
we shall end our day.
Will the whole journey be understood,
step by step of the way

Re-travelled, as your hand and mine
part, for the last time
forgiven and forgiving? . . . O then shine,
unrivalled, light from home!

Unpublished and Uncollected Poems

The Silver Sea

This very night the dark plain of the sea
has broken again into silver. I would have run,
body and spirit taut with the one joy,
to swim again towards that memoried moon.

Spirit of life, my lover, master, friend,
desert me. Be not faithful like the sea,
the moon, forever returning rhythmic powers.
In depth of dark I'll see reality.

How long must the vision of the world of light
by which I lived, source of my love, endure?
That world I knew. This, is unlearnt,
where death, I'm told, dowses every fire.

Though I know not this life, this death, I know
the Spirit moving over that silver sea,
breathing on the darling treasures of my slave heart
that seem eternally indestructible in me.

My lover is too faithful. Leaves me lost,
verging the chasm where none but the lost may seek,
and then – half-heard half-felt that nameless voice
far, near, summons me back.

So at this last, to you I'll release my battering love,
Spirit of life, that it may spring to your call
in straight flight home to the world of light –
forsaken, forgotten, its jailer and its cell.

The Door

I lived the waiting years,
door set wide,
lamp, with moon and stars,
for the wanderer's guide –

My lavish bread, remorse.
My drink, despair.
Threshold shadows from the moon
to mock my prayer.

But the deepening labyrinth of time
echoed with the grief
of all such love as mine,
severed, not by death but life.

And barred now is my door
against the accusing host
of the beautiful, the wise, the good,
from the encircling past.

Reasonable Questions at Selected Stages

When the children's angels from the warm upper air
Dropped, they slept
In this deep grass, shared
With these lizards. Who then feared?
Who at a distance kept?

When that Lion sun of summer-without-end
Broke his word,
Did the Lord of Life not send
The Christmas child to defend
The sleep of angel and lizard?

That vixen, alone on the velvet apricot snow,
Who at some apt sign
Capered and pranced as though
Flicked by laughter – did she know
Secular laughter from divine?

If all deaths end in boundless death
As rivers in the sea
Or stars diving into the depth
Of a first August; whose faith
Will be the faith that is music, is poetry,

And which whilst mingled flowing burning water light
Conclude their calm
Homeward course, will articulate
Resurging passion? Who will recreate
For the music, musician; poet, for the poem?

(This poem seems to recapitulate the themes of 'Death in
the Snow' and many other poems of the Plash Mill period.
It was to have been included in *All in the Day's Work*.)

This Journey
Must be Gone Alone and by Night

'Give me a handful of stars
To light each seventh mile,
And I'll never mind the dark, the dark
Which I'll learn to know well!'

'You shall have both moon and stars
For every seventh mile,
And the rest of the way will be dark with the dark
Which none knows well.'

Finding a surefoot path
By imagined light ahead,
She cried: 'Hurrah for the dark, the dark
Of which fool hearts are afraid!

'Already the arch of heaven
Gleams with the Holy Ghost!'
That first seventh she danced away
Beneath a jewelled host,

Whilst the voices of moon and stars
And the voices of rivers and sea
Met and mingled, rose and fell,
Through time to eternity.

Now silent, spent, by the dark
Miles dragged along
From each glimmering space into dark,
She builds a dumb song.

(This poem was to have been included in *All in the Day's Work*)

'That which is past is to come,
That which comes is past,
Unfaltering rhythm neither finds
Nor seeks rest.

'Christ! May the ultimate dark,
The ultimate light,
End soon this endlessness, and merge,
Cancelled out.'

Question and Answer

Weightless over the snow,
Soundless, fleeting, wild,
Whose shadow passes, checks, is gone,
Unnamed as a stillborn child?

Bang the door, you fool.
Slam shutters. Goad the fire.
None comes this way tonight or any night
For all your prayer.

After Many Years

'Could I ever forget?' said Lazarus.
No, he could never forget.
'The touch of the grass,' said Lazarus,
'Cool, and shiny wet.
I'd been so certain I'd never feel it again —
I'd wept.'

'I was young, you know,' said Lazarus.
'But after all I did have to die —
His dying was my lasting death,
Mine, his agony . . .
I've never lived since,' said Lazarus,
'Except in that memory.'

'But he rose from death,' they soothed.
'He touched again the grass.
Agony ends, is extinguished.
The unendurable must pass.
It's life that is everlasting —
He proved that, Lazarus.'

'Has *he* ever forgotten?' cried Lazarus.
Questions that love asks death
Bring their own tumult of echoes,
And, caught on some listening breath,
Clear as bells, an answer . . . .
No, he will never forget.

Penwith

Every night and all night, pressing against the pane –
What, who, is out there, soundless, staring in?
Curtain closely drawn, for I dare not, dare not, look,
I crouch at room's length near the fire – *'not here whom ye seek.'*

Whether all night the fog-horns mourn for an inexpressible
    grief,
or the raging shouting tempest voices a dumbfound strife,
not a single night falls on the eternal moor and the sea
but strikes my flinching heart with terror of the vigil's
    mystery.

Could it be the one in need? One of whom my need is great?
Never shall I know in truth, lacking sound or sight.
One who has roamed unresting for centuries, seeker or lost?
The moor was trodden, mine worked, before Jesus Christ.

Every night and all night. Only the moor?
Nothing the moor demanded has ever caused me fear.
That Fearless Spirit I once knew and worshipped would
    fling back
the curtain, though it cover the last sight on which I'll look.

Every night and all night unseeing and seen.
Futile curtain, fire's a beacon, lamp's a moon.
Frequent now the thought, *is it I myself who come
captive of the moor, to watch the haunted stranger in my home?*

Remembering An Unanswered Prayer

(Later called *Prayer*)

Can any find what is lost?
Never, never.
Yet some search with their hearts
For ever, ever.

Then, it was I who was lost,
climbing Caradon
violet under sunset snow
above my valley of stone.

'Mary whose son was lost,
with your mantle hide
the betrayings of my coward feet,
and bury this dead.'

Needless To Say I Was Alone

Needless to say I was alone
When the messenger came,
Night unthreatened by dawn
Wrapping dreamer and dream,

And the dream all of innocence,
Of the innocent dead
And their endless unwilled influence
Through the stained steadfast blood.

Then the listener to the thudding stream
Out in the windless dark
Knew no further dawn must come
To separate heart from heart.

The kingdom's here, I thought,
My lifted eyes
Watching the room melt
Into death's dark paradise.

But the spider held her breath
Against the appalling change
And the garnet glare of the moth
Withdrew from the pane

As the living fire in the grate
Ghost-grey fell
And the lamp's flower of light
Sank on the wall.

O darkness be my sun!
Cried my heart, nor feared
The thudding stream, the blood,
The unwilled Word.

Then a hand lifted the latch
And one stood there
Darker than darkness. Such
A silent messenger

Never had come my way
Who in wild bravado cried:
'Come to go? To stay?
Living? Or dead?'

Never an answering word,
Never a sound,
Until over the fields stirred
The small wolf-wind

And light opened the east
Behind that messenger
Who for all I know was a holy ghost
Or comforter.

At This Distance

At this distance I view everything
equally with, and without, partiality.
Am seeker, lost. Judge, accused.
Innocent, guilty.

I am concerned to remain at this distance
where all cancels all.
Nothingness is my choice, if choice be granted
the inaudible and invisible.

Spirit of the encircling world of light,
annul my senses lest they hear and see!
Silent, I invoke your nameless Name
against contagion with infinity.